I0816440

THE ART OF
GODZILLA x KONG
THE NEW EMPIRE

THE ART OF GODZILLA x KONG: THE NEW EMPIRE

WRITTEN BY JAMES MOTTRAM

FOREWORD BY TOM HAMMOCK

INTRODUCTION BY ADAM WINGARD

LEGENDARY

INSIGHT EDITIONS

SAN RAFAEL • LOS ANGELES • LONDON

cont

ents

FOREWORD
BY TOM HAMMOCK

I love these "Art of" books and remember a time spent waiting for them to come out for favorite films, and then poring through them, studying every detail in the art. Adam Wingard and I agonized over what to include in this book. The road not taken and finding out how something came to be is often as interesting as hero illustrations. We have tried to present a mix of image types to share our process with you.

As the cast and crew began to come together to make this film, Adam and I watched a fascinating thing happen; people would ask each other about the first time they saw a Godzilla or King Kong film. It happened organically, and yet this became a rite of passage, a way to break the ice for crew members. An instant bond. For so many people, the question evoked a deep memory: An uncle had taken them to a rundown repertory cinema to see *Godzilla*; a grandmother had shown them *King Kong* on her old television that was as deep as it was wide; teenage friends had stumbled across a Titan film on late-night television. It didn't matter where we were working in the world—Iceland, Australia, Brazil—this question became the ritual. Everyone had a story. These two Titans are so ingrained in worldwide culture, so beloved. That love brought this team of artists together. It's their amazing work we're going to celebrate in this book.

As the team of artists began to coalesce, we began revisiting the world of *Godzilla vs. Kong*, but that world had changed. Monarch had looked to the future, and we were going to get to visit the farthest reaches of Hollow Earth to tell this story. Adam and I always look to place and color when we start working together on a film, no matter the scale. Color for the film became the memory of a trip down an '80s toy aisle. We decided to lean into that color palette both for Monarch and for Hollow Earth—but the dirty, scratched, lived-in version of that palette.

From the earliest days of our decade-long collaboration, Adam has focused on achieving as much in-camera as possible during production. We approached the visuals with the idea that again, as on *Godzilla vs. Kong*, we would go around the world to make the film. We used the art to communicate that approach, always starting with an image of a real place and then building off of it. You'll see all of these real locations represented in the art. Within these illustrations, we were working visually toward a production plan that would allow us to take the audience to the deserts of Morocco, the glaciers of Iceland, the jungles of Australia, the ruins of Rome, and the beaches of Rio de Janeiro. It's no small thing, but Adam was totally committed. Give the Titans a world rooted in reality, and they become that much more real.

And those Titans. Adam wanted to try something new and put the Titans front and center in the tale—give them a story arc of their own. And for that, we needed new villains to balance out our heroes and round out our Hollow Earth ecosystem—one worthy of Kong and one worthy of Godzilla. The process to come to these new Titan characters was long, and rooted in both nature and myth. It constantly amazed me to see the passion people have for these Titans as they progressed from pencil through paintings and into the world of digital models. It was equally rewarding for the crew to see these new Titans come to life. We hope you love them as much as we do.

With that, we headed out into the world to make this film. Ultimately, a film is many tiny decisions made by a huge number of amazing artists that add up to a whole. So many wonderful people came together to make this film. It's a special thing to get to revisit a movie for a sequel, and to revisit a cinematic world with friends. Adam and I hope that this book has given some insight into the process, and that seeing *Godzilla x Kong* created some great memories for you, whether it's your first Titan film or your 40th.

Enjoy,
Tom

PAGE 2 In the midst of a rematch, as depicted by Manuel Plank-Jorge, Godzilla and Kong tower over the rooftops of a Cairo suburb.
PREVIOUS PAGES Wart Dogs pursue Kong in this concept piece by Matt Allsopp.
OPPOSITE Production designer Tom Hammock on the set of *The New Empire*.

H.E.A.V. M.U.L.E.
OPERATOR'S MANUAL

INTRODUCTION
BY ADAM WINGARD

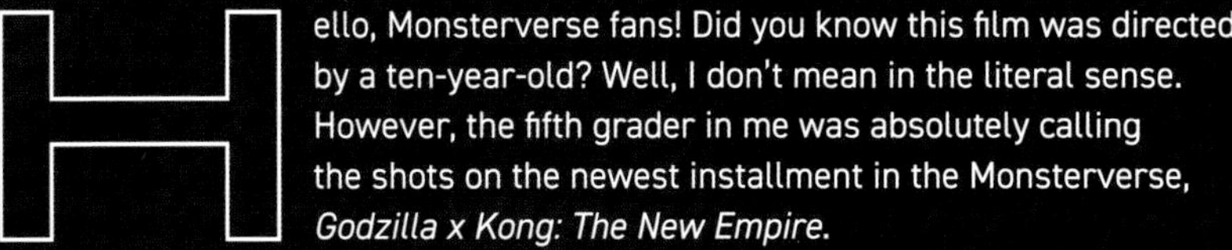

Hello, Monsterverse fans! Did you know this film was directed by a ten-year-old? Well, I don't mean in the literal sense. However, the fifth grader in me was absolutely calling the shots on the newest installment in the Monsterverse, *Godzilla x Kong: The New Empire*.

Throughout my career, it has been my personal quest to unearth the original spark of my childhood influences. My tendency has been to satisfy my inner child, catering to all his desires and whims, creating things I could only dream of as an aspiring director. When I created *You're Next* and *The Guest*, that was for sixteen-year-old Adam—the teenager who was obsessed with all things action, horror, and sci-fi (particularly the R-rated ones, of course). When I create the Godzilla-and-Kong movies, the ten-year-old within who would catch every monster movie on daytime television takes over like a Blatty-style exorcism.

In *Godzilla vs. Kong*, we pushed the color palette into a vivid, '80s-style neon tone—especially in the latter half, which took place in the vibrant city of Hong Kong. For the sequel, I wanted to go further—bringing in my own experience of strolling down the toy aisles in the '80s. If you are too young to remember what this was like, I must say, you've regrettably missed out. It was an overload of splashy, brilliant neon colors on every shelf: Thundercats, G.I. Joe, Transformers, Masters of the Universe—all the classics were there, and each box featured incredible artwork that was designed to be a cognitive color overload. This visual assault of the senses was forever embedded into my mind, and this film became the perfect outlet for that particular inspiration.

Godzilla x Kong: The New Empire represents my sixth feature film collaboration with production designer Tom Hammock. Without him and his accomplished assemblage of artists, I would not have been able to bring this madness to life. Tom is masterful in his approach to stylized concepts such as this; he always finds a way to make things happen and balances both the establishing and implementing of my most insane ideas. His ability to do so is crucial to the production; anyone can put something wild and colorful on the screen, but only someone with his skills to create a solid foundation to build from can make it believable and grounded—or at least as grounded as a zero-gravity realm thousands of miles below the Earth's surface can be.

In the last film, we took a short tour of Hollow Earth. In this film, we actually get to live there and fully experience this unreal, lost-in-time environment. Having the capability to expand Kong's domain was a huge factor in my decision to return to direct another Monsterverse film, and I am pleased to say the results have far exceeded my expectations going in. I have always maintained that making these films is putting pure imagination on display, and that holds strong as the perfect articulation of my experience.

Here's to PURE IMAGINATION, and to all the incredible artists and the tireless effort that makes this all possible—without them, imagination is just a dream.

LEFT: Adam Wingard on set performing his cameo as the M.U.L.E. operator.

acknowledgments

In bringing *Godzilla x Kong: The New Empire* to the big screen, the success of this cinematic spectacle rests not only on the shoulders of the iconic monsters themselves but also on the dedicated efforts of an extraordinary team of individuals. A remarkable crew with tireless commitment, creativity, and expertise helped bring every frame of this epic adventure to life. Our deepest appreciation goes to the talented artists and designers who crafted the awe-inspiring visuals of the film. Emily Seresin and her team, whose stunningly realized costumes helped our actors embody their characters in a grounded reality. Translating the intricate concept art into breathtaking sequences, each frame of the film is a testament to the boundless imagination and technical prowess of our Visual Effects department. Alessandro Ongaro and Tom Elder-Groebe, along with partners at WETA, DNEG, Scanline, Luma, Supervixen, The Third Floor and Legacy brought the iconic monsters to life and imbued the world of *Godzilla x Kong: The New Empire* with depth, richness, and authenticity.

A dedicated production team, led by Eric Mcleod, Jen Conry, and 1st Assistant Director Brian Galligan, whose meticulous planning and coordination ensured the seamless execution of every aspect of the film. Along with crews in Australia, Italy, Morocco, Brazil, Hawaii, Gibraltar, Spain, and Iceland, their tireless efforts behind the scenes were instrumental in overcoming countless challenges and bringing the ambitious vision of *Godzilla x Kong: The New Empire* to fruition.

Special acknowledgment is due to the passionate fans whose unwavering support and enthusiasm fueled our journey from the earliest stages of development to the final release. Your passion is the lifeblood of the Monsterverse, and we are endlessly grateful for your continued support.

Last but certainly not least, we extend our heartfelt appreciation to the countless unsung heroes whose contributions, both big and small, played an integral role in the creation of *Godzilla x Kong: The New Empire.* To the people at Legendary Entertainment, from the Creative Department to Physical Production and everyone involved in Post-Production and Marketing, it takes a passionate village to get these movies made, and we could not do it without everyone's dedication and expertise.

OPPOSITE The cast and crew of *Godzilla x Kong: The New Empire* poses on the set near the end of principal photography.

V6
V10

PART I

THE NEW EMPIRE

PART I:

THE NEW EMPIRE

When director Adam Wingard was coming to the end of making his 2021 film *Godzilla vs. Kong*, his mind turned to what to do next. He admits the idea of creating another entry for the Monsterverse, Legendary's film franchise that has brought together such Titans of cinema as Godzilla and Kong, exhausted him. "Initially, my reaction was, 'This is such a big undertaking, it's hard to imagine doing another one of these big monster movies again,'" Wingard says.

As he got thinking, however, Wingard remembered an interview he'd read with fellow filmmaker Quentin Tarantino. In it, the interviewer asked why Tarantino had made back-to-back westerns with *Django Unchained* (2012) and *The Hateful Eight* (2015). "[Tarantino] said that he just figured out how to make a western, how to shoot people on horses—and it was a shame not to go on and put those skills to the test with another western."

Wingard felt the same about making another Monsterverse movie. "I just had figured out how to do a movie with so much VFX that now I felt like, 'OK, I know how to apply this, and I know how to do it better,'" he says. It wasn't just a case of doing it better; it was also a matter of pushing the boundaries of what computer-rendered characters like Godzilla and Kong were capable of. "The main thing that I wanted to do on this film was lean more into the effects and into the monsters as characters," Wingard adds.

Despite this desire to test the capabilities of VFX, as he had done on *Godzilla vs. Kong*, Wingard was committed to shooting in-camera as much as possible to ground these fantastical creatures in real-world environments. "There was a given that a certain amount of the film had to be completely CGI," he says, "but it made it all the more important that we get as many real exotic locations in front of the camera and put the characters into those as much as possible."

The moment he committed to making the film, he contacted screenwriters Terry Rossio, who had cowritten *Godzilla vs. Kong*, and Simon Barrett, his longtime collaborator on his lower-budget horror hits like *You're Next* (2011), *The Guest* (2014), and *Blair Witch* (2016). "I kind of told them both . . . the way I see this picture is that it's an experimental movie in a lot of ways," says Wingard. "And it's a movie that's going to rely on large, long sequences of nonverbal storytelling."

PREVIOUS PAGES Kong, wielding his axe, comes to blows with the Skar King in zero gravity in this piece by Matt Allsopp.
RIGHT In this illustration by Matt Allsopp, the Skar King is pulling no punches as he battles Kong in zero gravity.

KING OF THE CALORIES
MIKE'S MONSTERS
REDDO SQUAD
C♥S
NO MORE! I'M SICK OF GODZILLA!!!
RED BAMBO
MONARCH LIES!

Wingard was well aware that a word like "experimental" might scare studio executives, but with all the experience he'd gathered from his time on *Godzilla vs. Kong*, he felt it was the right approach. "We're not just making another monster movie, we're making a monster character study," he says. "We're letting the monsters tell their own story. And we're going to do it in a way that doesn't rely on dialogue. And so that was the last time we called the movie 'experimental.' But we all knew that that's really what we were making. And then we jumped in."

Beginning with the working title *Origins*, *Godzilla x Kong: The New Empire*, as it would ultimately be called, was underway.

Nevertheless, Wingard's story would deliberately keep Kong and Godzilla apart for much of the narrative and lean more toward Kong as the main character. "In this movie, it was always going to be Kong's story," says Wingard. "And Godzilla is a part of it. *Godzilla vs. Kong* was both of their films. That's why that film was split into two storylines—one for Godzilla, one for Kong. This one's definitely Kong's story."

At the start of *The New Empire*, Kong is now deep in Hollow Earth, the ancient ecosystem close to the planet's core introduced in *Kong: Skull Island* (2017), directed by Jordan Vogt-Roberts. While Wingard had explored it in his earlier Monsterverse movie, he was keen to return. "Hollow Earth was a gimme," he says. "We knew that we were going to spend a lot of time there. And that's completely a place where we could just let our imagination run wild."

With Jeremy Slater, a cowriter on *Fantastic Four* (2015) and creator of the Marvel TV show *Moon Knight* (2022), also recruited to work on the script, Wingard and his screenwriters didn't want to confine the story just to Hollow Earth. "These movies are such a worldwide phenomenon, and so you want to give that global feel to it, as a starting point," says Wingard. "Even though the origins [of Kong and Godzilla] are from America and from Japan, these are characters that I think everybody's taken ownership of, to a certain degree. And so, you want to really give that feeling—these characters really are all over the planet—and just give it that scope."

LEFT This illustration by Christian Gonzalez explores a concept for Godzilla graffiti in Rome.

While *Godzilla vs. Kong* ferried audiences from the snowy wilderness of Antarctica to the sleek high-rises of Hong Kong, Wingard had new ideas for *The New Empire*. Wingard began thinking of setting the film in some of the world's most iconic locations, from Rio de Janeiro to the Colosseum in Rome and the pyramids in Egypt. "It's always most interesting to see the monsters depicted against backdrops that you know and can relate to so that when you see them next to it, it really imprints on you," he says.

As the story grew, Wingard says, he was "developing it from a very visual standpoint" in his mind. He wanted to paint it in bright colors, the primary hues he remembered from 1980s cartoons and toys. "All the eye candy, the colors that you would see as a kid, impressed upon me in a way where I wanted to bring that to one of these films," he says. From very early on, he began discussing the palette with production designer Tom Hammock, who had worked with Wingard on *Godzilla vs. Kong*.

"When it came to color, what Adam and I were thinking is that these blockbuster movies, to a certain extent, they all share a similar look," says Hammock. "We wanted to do something that's more like when you walked down the Walmart toy aisle in the '80s . . ."

As bright as he intended the film to be, Wingard also felt that it needed to feel grounded. "You want to always believe that these monsters are real," he says. "And so I wanted to do something where I was taking a very stylized reality, very colorful reality, and similarly bringing it to life in a way that you've never seen. Because normally, whenever things are stylized in kind of an '80s cartoon way, they tend to be a lot more fantastic and not grounded, so, from a distance, it almost looks like a toy playset. But when you get closer to it, you see all the wear and tear."

With this visual mission in mind, the plot began to take shape. No longer in his natural habitat of Skull Island, Kong has been scouring Hollow Earth in vain for his own kind, and his isolation there has left him feeling low. The same can be said for Jia (Kaylee Hottle), an orphaned girl who grew up on Skull Island as part of the ancient Iwi tribe, and who was adopted by Dr. Ilene Andrews (Rebecca Hall), Chief Science Officer at Monarch, the highly equipped cryptozoological agency at the heart of the Monsterverse. The two reside on a Monarch base in Barbados, close to the Hollow Earth Access Point, which leads directly into this world within our own. Jia, who is deaf, can communicate with Kong via sign language, which helps to cement their unique bond.

Wingard says he sees Jia and Kong's journeys as parallel: "They're both kind of going through the same existential crisis and discovery period. They're both afloat without anyone necessarily to relate to. They both feel adrift and lonely, and out of place, out of sorts in the world. One of the things that I learned the most on the last film is that to tell the monster story, the human story has to perfectly reflect it in its own way to understand the monsters. It has to be from an emotional perspective."

Distracted and unsettled, Jia has been creating drawings at school—ominous black triangle shapes—that echo patterns of interference radiating from Hollow Earth. A distress signal, coded in an ancient language, seems to be calling her. Andrews realizes they need to journey into Hollow Earth to discover more. Joining them is Bernie Hayes (Brian Tyree Henry), the Titan expert and conspiracy theorist, last seen helping take down Mechagodzilla, the biomechanical terror that rampaged through Hong Kong in the finale of *Godzilla vs. Kong*.

The mission also calls for the arrival of a newcomer, Trapper (Dan Stevens), a daredevil veterinarian who knows Andrews from their college days. "In a lot of ways, all the characters in the movie, Trapper and Bernie included, are these outcast characters who don't necessarily belong," explains Wingard. "Where they belong is on an adventure." And an adventure is exactly what they get. As the film's heroes work their way through the wild flora and fauna of Hollow Earth, they discover ancient Iwi ruins and a lost civilization that Jia belongs to.

In tandem with this adventure, Kong meets Suko, a mischievous ape that initially tries to lead Kong to his doom. Riffing on the son of Kong idea, Wingard felt he had what he calls "the vibe" of the character. "[Suko] could bite your face off. Like, he's cute, but he's also kind of ferocious and formidable in his own little way." Kong soon discovers that Suko belongs to a race of Great Apes enslaved in a lava-filled part of Hollow Earth.

Ruling these apes with utter brutality is the Skar King, a malevolent, red-hued creature who is another character who materialized early in Wingard's mind. "I knew who the villain was," he says. "I knew that I wanted there to be an archnemesis to Kong that ended up being the Skar King. I knew I wanted him to be cherry red." So powerful is the Skar King that he holds a Titan as his prisoner—the ice-breathing world ender Shimo, "a living weapon of mass destruction," as Wingard calls her.

Meanwhile, Godzilla, anticipating a battle with Shimo and the Skar King, has rejuvenated himself. After defeating Scylla, a crab-like creature with deadly claws, in Rome, he curls up in one of the city's most iconic landmarks, the Colosseum, to recuperate before making his way to the ocean. Swimming toward Arctic waters, Godzilla battles the serpent-like Tiamat in pursuit of energy reserves, which he uses to metamorphose into a battle-hardened version of himself. As he awakens, alerted by the activity in Hollow Earth, a turf war brews between these Titans—one destined to erupt on the planet's surface.

Wingard resolved to pit the massive creatures of the Monsterverse against one another. If Shimo is the archnemesis to Godzilla, the Skar King is Kong's. "I knew that I wanted the Skar King to have enslaved all these Great Apes, and it was up to Kong to [free them] and step into his own place and really take his crown," he says.

OPPOSITE Zero-gravity battle with opal boulders by Matt Allsopp.

PART II

THE TITANS

PART II:
THE TITANS

As the script began to come together for *Godzilla x Kong: The New Empire*, the production was already moving forward with design elements. Wingard has always been a fan of the grounded look of the Titans in the Monsterverse, compared to those seen in other Hollywood creature features where the influence of famed fantasy writer H. P. Lovecraft's bizarre creations is perhaps too strong. "For me, in the Monsterverse, the difference is that the monsters always have a much more simplistic relatability, so Godzilla resembles a dinosaur lizard in his own way, Kong, obviously an ape, and so forth," says Wingard.

Alongside Wingard, steering the design aesthetic was Tom Hammock, the film's production designer, who was in charge of inspiring his army of concept illustrators to delve into their imaginations to create *The New Empire*'s new Titans. The familiar Godzilla and Kong may be the leads, but the expansive storyline was filled with far more beasts—ranging from the Skar King to Suko, Mothra, and Shimo—than in any previous Monsterverse movie.

Instrumental in the creature design phase was Legacy Effects, the esteemed special effects company whose credits include the three previous Godzilla outings in the Monsterverse. Concept illustrator Jared Krichevsky remembers Wingard sitting down with the Legacy team to pitch the whole story, hinting that size really is everything: "We were just excited to be back with [Wingard] again."

Realism played a part too, however. Suko, for example, went through various stages of evolution. "We experimented with being closer to a chimp look, experimented with being closer to a Great Ape look. There were some early orangutan experiments too," says Hammock. "You want Suko to be cute. But you also want him to be a little shit!" Likewise, the Skar King was inspired by Mother Nature. "There's this really creepy group of [real-life] chimps that hunt other chimps," adds Hammock. "And so we really started looking at them, and specifically their facial expressions. And that was really the basis for the Skar King."

The more fantastical Shimo, a Titan to rival Godzilla, came from Wingard's desire to push the boundaries of VFX, creating a creature with a pearlescent quality to its skin. "I didn't want her to just be another monster with a leathery hide," says Wingard. "Depending on where the light's hitting it, I wanted it to have that shimmer like gasoline does."

Wingard was also desperate to bring back fan-favorite Mothra, a Titan who previously appeared in *Godzilla: King of the Monsters* (2019) but died by the film's conclusion. "When *King of the Monsters* came out, my dad went to go see the movie, and the first thing he said was how much he loved Mothra. And that always stuck with me. That was a character that just instantly, people loved. The other Titans, you want to see them pounding into each other; Mothra is more of an ethereal presence, which we needed in this movie."

Ultimately, Wingard identified a narrative thread that would bring Mothra's species back into the Monsterverse while also expanding the franchise's lore. As Wingard explains, "This is essentially Mothra's mother . . . "The eggs that were laid on the surface were laid by [*The New Empire*'s version of Mothra], and this film establishes that [she] is the protector of the pathways to the surface, which are these vortexes. And so, theoretically, [this Titan] has access to these vortexes and laid eggs on the surface, which is what we saw in *King of the Monsters*. [She] is the OG one."

PREVIOUS PAGES "This was a lush, green, prehistoric environment to give a sense of beauty without the danger of the [Skar King's] red colors," says illustrator Michele Moen. "Kong shows surprise at discovering Suko, and Suko is a little shy and tentative at meeting Kong. The expressions on both Kong and Suko were very important."
OPPOSITE An injured Kong clutches his arm in pain in this illustration by Moen.

KONG

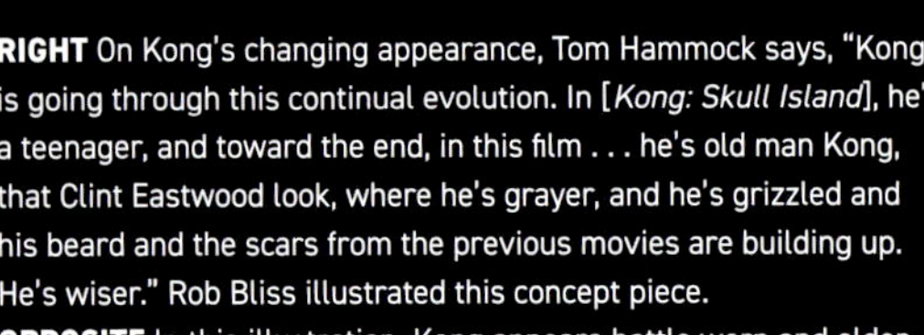

RIGHT On Kong's changing appearance, Tom Hammock says, "Kong is going through this continual evolution. In [*Kong: Skull Island*], he's a teenager, and toward the end, in this film . . . he's old man Kong, that Clint Eastwood look, where he's grayer, and he's grizzled and his beard and the scars from the previous movies are building up. He's wiser." Rob Bliss illustrated this concept piece.
OPPOSITE In this illustration, Kong appears battle worn and older than in previous Monsterverse films.

SUKO

OPPOSITE LEFT Suko, featuring a red stripe that shows his allegiance to the Skar King, as depicted by illustrator Jared Krichevsky.
LEFT AND OPPOSITE RIGHT Regarding Suko's design, illustrator Rob Bliss says, "I was very definitely trying to keep it as chimp-like as possible . . . to make him a cute and sympathetic kind of character. One that people would emote over. So that's probably why I've got such sparkly eyes and why the face is so important."
ABOVE In this concept by Simon Webber, Suko bears a scar that alludes to his rough life growing up under the Skar King's rule.

THIS PAGE Designs by the team at Wētā Workshop show studies of Suko inspired by a chimpanzee. "You want Suko to be a character—so, a bit of a preteen—but he can't be too bratty, or you don't like him," says Tom Hammock. "You want his eyes to be big and sympathetic, but not ridiculously big. So he's cute, but not too cute. We wanted him to be a mini Kong, but it took a long time to get to that place where everyone felt, 'That's the one—we can see his character.'"

OPPOSITE Early concept art by Rob Bliss shows Kong and Suko together. The version of young Suko being explored here ... more developed physically

OPPOSITE "Mothra was always a character I imprinted on a lot as a kid. Mothra is the only character that really has this truce with Godzilla or this partnership in the way that they do. And so it felt right that Mothra would come back for this one. It felt like she needed to," says Adam Wingard. "That's really the only way that you can communicate with Godzilla. Kong, he can half-communicate with Godzilla, but, really, he can't get the whole thing out. He needs Mothra's help to really seal the deal."

LEFT AND BELOW LEFT Mothra's new look as realized by Scanline VFX.

BELOW A close-up on Mothra's face. "The character design itself was very much a continuation of what was established by [Michael] Dougherty in [*Godzilla: King of the Monsters*]."

THE SKAR KING

THESE PAGES In these early concepts by Simon Webber, the Skar King is pictured with a headdress crafted from an animal skull. Eventually, the Skar King's design included a whip fashioned from animal bones, dubbed the Whipslash, an indicator of the character's brutality. In the illustration to the right, a human figure can be seen in the foreground, offering a sense of the Skar King's incredible scale.

OPPOSITE A trio of Skar King concepts by Jared Krichevsky. "I thought it would be fun to play with a weird shape that would stand out and make him really unique. I just wanted to play with big hair!" says Krichevsky. These concepts include the Skar King's Whipslash—a whip made from the vertebrae of a fallen enemy. **THIS PAGE** This pair of concepts by Simon Webber depicts the Skar King in action, showcasing his longer limbs, which were designed to endow him with a different fighting style from Kong's.

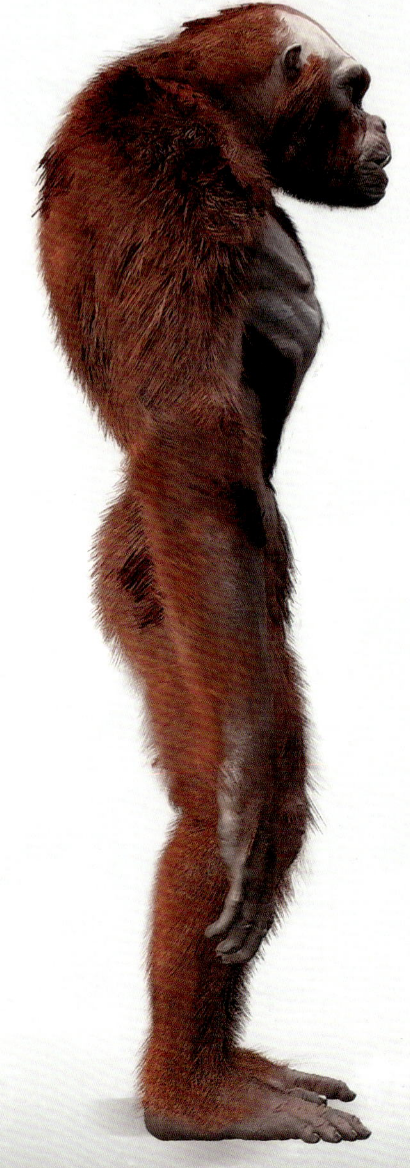

OPPOSITE The final look of the Skar King by Wētā Workshop.
LEFT The Skar King strikes a pose in this piece by Wētā Workshop. The cruel tyrant's Whipslash, which he uses to subdue opponents and even control Shimo through one of her crystals at the tip, survived through multiple iterations of the character.

SHIMO

OPPOSITE On the subtle details of Shimo's design, Jared Krichevsky explained that "Adam [Wingard] had mentioned, 'What if [Shimo] was drooling?' So the drool was freezing on [Shimo's] face." Also showcased are the Hollow Earth crystals that Shimo fused with during her long hibernation underground.
ABOVE An iteration of Shimo with a more alligator-like head, courtesy of Krichevsky. Shimo's pearlescent skin was designed to shimmer like a crystal of ice.
LEFT Dragons, crocodiles, and triceratops all feed into this trio of designs, each a riff on various ideas for Shimo by Rob Bliss.

ABOVE LEFT This Shimo concept by Simon Webber features glowing turquois eyes and a wise, Old Man Winter look, ideas that were discarded in the final design.
TOP LEFT AND ABOVE RIGHT These two illustrations by Webber show Shimo in the Arctic, with Chinook helicopters highlighting the enormous scale of the creature.
TOP RIGHT One of Jared Krichevsky's early iterations of Shimo, featuring a prominent underbite.
OPPOSITE "They wanted the ice spikes to make that arc on the way

LEFT The final look of Shimo as depicted by Jared Krichevsky.
RIGHT "For her ice breath, I was thinking like dry ice. It's foggy and thick. But there's a little bit of glow behind it," says Krichevsky.

DROWNVIPER

OPPOSITE Hoping to ditch Kong, Suko leads him to a lagoon where a serpent-like creature awaits. In this illustration by Michele Moen, Kong seemingly dispatches the creature with ease.

THIS PAGE Three designs for the Drownviper by Wētā Workshop's Alex Ries. Inspired by photorealistic dinosaur-themed books he read when he was young, Adam Wingard wanted this vicious-looking beast to look grounded. "To me, the key to the Monsterverse Titans is that there is a simplicity to the design. We wanted this to be an evolved version of an eel. Something relatable to our reality. The basis for all our creature designs is that the Hollow Earth ecosystem and the surface ecosystem are closely aligned and thus the animals should be as well," he says.

Vertacines

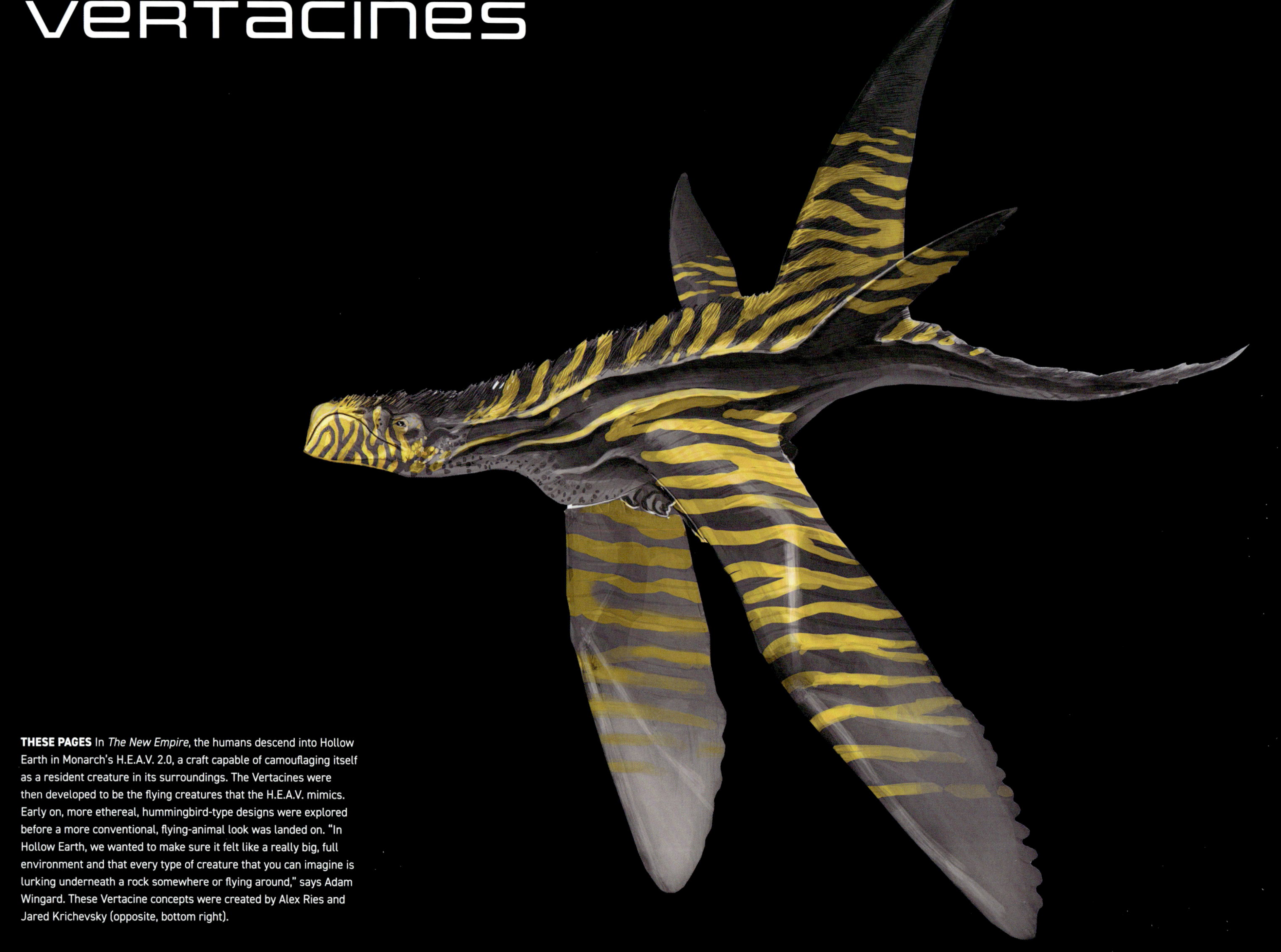

THESE PAGES In *The New Empire*, the humans descend into Hollow Earth in Monarch's H.E.A.V. 2.0, a craft capable of camouflaging itself as a resident creature in its surroundings. The Vertacines were then developed to be the flying creatures that the H.E.A.V. mimics. Early on, more ethereal, hummingbird-type designs were explored before a more conventional, flying-animal look was landed on. "In Hollow Earth, we wanted to make sure it felt like a really big, full environment and that every type of creature that you can imagine is lurking underneath a rock somewhere or flying around," says Adam Wingard. These Vertacine concepts were created by Alex Ries and Jared Krichevsky (opposite, bottom right).

HOLLOW EARTH FAUNA

ABOVE AND RIGHT Affectionately nicknamed Fly Guy by the crew of *The New Empire*, this creature comes courtesy of the Wētā Workshop team. Adam Wingard decided to utilize the design for an insect that Jia sees at an Iwi Temple, ultimately leading her to Mothra. "This creature is an envoy for Mothra, almost like a real fairy in some ways, interfacing with Jia and taking her deeper to where she needs to be," says Wingard. "We worked at exploring the ecosystem on Hollow Earth in even the smallest animals."
OPPOSITE A set of concepts by Alex Ries and Jared Krichevsky (bottom) for another Hollow Earth resident, the parrot frog. "The parrot frog came from studying howler monkeys in South America. They are tiny monkeys, but apparently, it's only the great whales that produce a larger volume of sound," says Tom Hammock. "So we had the idea of, what if you have this tiny frog that's making a huge [Kong-like] sound, and it's confusing Kong? It adds to his loneliness at that moment."

PART III

HEROES OF HOLLOW EARTH

PART III:
HEROES OF HOLLOW EARTH

In *Godzilla x Kong: The New Empire*, the story picks up the fates of not only the two titular Titans but also the human characters around them. At the center is Dr. Ilene Andrews, played once again by British actor Rebecca Hall. Since *Godzilla vs. Kong*, Monarch's Chief Science Officer has become the adoptive mother of Jia, an Iwi girl, with actor Kaylee Hottle reprising her role. "[Jia is] the lead of the movie from the human standpoint," says Wingard. As she journeys to Hollow Earth, she not only finds her people but also discovers her destiny. "She becomes an Iwi shaman," the director adds. "And that's how I saw Jia, ultimately. She's the monster whisperer—she's able to communicate directly with the Titans."

The team Andrews assembles includes conspiracy theorist Bernie Hayes, host of the *Titan Truth* podcast, played by the returning Brian Tyree Henry. Following the events in Hong Kong, his reputation has been trashed after Monarch didn't confirm his involvement in taking down Mechagodzilla. "You get more of Bernie in his element than you did in the last movie," says Wingard. "Who is this conspiracy guy? What does his place look like?"

Joining the gang is Trapper, a maverick vet introduced to audiences when Kong surfaces from Hollow Earth with a broken tooth. Wingard cast Dan Stevens, who previously starred as a dashing but sinister killer in his film *The Guest*. "I wanted a lead in this movie that was your cool leading man but wasn't boring in the way that leading men can be boring!" says Wingard. "I wanted all of the attributes that Dan is best at to come to the surface with the character."

Other newcomers to the Monsterverse include Mikhail, a Monarch employee who accompanies the group into Hollow Earth. Wingard knew exactly who he wanted to cast: Alex Ferns, the Scottish character actor who had a memorable role in the HBO drama *Chernobyl* (2019) as miner Andrei Glukhov. "I felt like his ability to play these intense, grumpy characters is just so unparalleled that he would be a great counterpoint to everybody else," notes Wingard.

Back on the surface is Hampton, the director of operations at the Monarch Barbados base. Wingard selected Rachel House, a New Zealand actor who lent her deadpan comedic chops to the role of Topaz in *Thor: Ragnarok* (2017). "We wanted to find somebody who was a little quirky, and that's why we went with Rachel," explains Wingard. "She's not what you would expect to be in this leadership role."

Rounding out the cast is Fala Chen, star of *Shang-Chi and the Legend of the Ten Rings* (2021), who portrays the Iwi Queen. "We knew that the person playing the Iwi Queen needed to have this gravitas and this compassion to her that would come through right away even without a spoken word, and Fala really got that and understood how to bring that quality to it, which isn't natural to most actors," Wingard says.

As much as casting was crucial, Wingard's innate ability to work with actors was also vital. "It was important to me that the actors really got along and had a real friendship that came across onscreen," he says. "I tried to create an environment so that the actors felt comfortable being able to realistically be a troupe of friends." With Andrews, Jia, and Bernie deciding to remain in Hollow Earth at the film's conclusion, *The New Empire* ends on a feel-good note. "This is a movie where it literally ends with everybody hugging it out. And you want an authentic camaraderie to come through," says Wingard.

Wingard had already learned sign language on *Godzilla vs. Kong*, helping him communicate with Hottle, who is deaf. But he took care with each cast member to learn their needs and methods on set, from those who like to do a lot of takes to those who prefer to nail it in one, as he looked to extract naturalistic performances from his players. "Everybody has their different way that they like to work," Wingard says. "And so my job as the director is to figure that out."

PREVIOUS PAGES Led by Trapper, the team explores the Hollow Earth jungle.
OPPOSITE The team poses under the ancient forest in Daintree, Australia, site of the oldest rainforest on Earth.

DR. ILENE ANDREWS

ABOVE The final Hollow Earth suit illustration for Ilene Andrews, played by Rebecca Hall. Illustrated by Imogene Chayes.
RIGHT As shown in this early concept by Jared Krichevsky, Dr. Ilene Andrews's mission suit was designed with a firefighter jumpsuit in mind, an outfit that could be put on swiftly, allowing her to be ready for action, according to costume designer Emily Seresin. "I wanted a design that spoke to utility and protection but that could also be

OPPOSITE Rebecca Hall on the jungle set at Village Roadshow Studios. The crew spent a year putting together their own nursery of prehistoric plants to be able to realistically populate the Hollow Earth jungle on stage.

JIA

THIS PAGE Two concept illustrations of Jia, played by Kaylee Hottle, illustrated by Imogene Chayes, designed by Emily Seresin. Visual changes reflect the character's move toward becoming a shamanlike figure among the Iwi people. Jia's donning of Iwi robes signaled the embrace of her heritage. "That moment seemed to call for grace and a lightness of touch befitting her youth and humility," says Seresin. **OPPOSITE** A photo by set decorator Thomas Salpietro showing the intense character detail in Jia's bedroom, including an origami Kong, a drawing of Kong, and clippings of butterflies, which foreshadow Jia's connection to Mothra

Linguistics Workbook
VOLUME 1
VOLUME 1
FLORA & FAUNA

Bernie Hayes

TOP An illustration by Alex Moy, depicting the hidden entrance to Bernie's apartment, envisioned as the back stairwell of a restaurant.
ABOVE AND OPPOSITE The interior of Bernie's apartment, illustrated by Moy. The above illustration features a notice board filled with conspiracy theory news clippings.
RIGHT Illustrator Marco Nelor depicts Bernie Hayes, played by Brian Tyree Henry, in his idiosyncratic outfit, complete with a vest covered with pins and the all-important fanny pack. "Bernie's vest was literally crammed with pins illustrating his personal obsessions and conspiracy theories. Adam liked the idea that it was Bernie's own personal mission suit," says costume designer Emily Seresin.

TRAPPER

ABOVE Trapper and Andrews on location on Morton Island, off the coast of Australia.
RIGHT On the design of Trapper, Adam Wingard says, "We modeled Trapper a little bit after some of the original G.I. Joe characters . . . we wanted to give him a lot more color and personality. He only wears his full mission look for one sequence in the movie. We immediately just had him take off the jacket because it didn't feel like it was right having Trapper cover up his signature Hawaiian- shirt look with a mission coat."
OPPOSITE Trapper in action on the M.U.L.E. set. According to costume designer Emily Seresin, "Trapper's shirt is printed with palm trees--it's the very opposite of camouflage. He has a

D2

MIKHAIL

ABOVE Mikhail on set in the Queensland, Australia, jungle, featuring the soundwave gun, designed by property master Steven B. Melton.
RIGHT Phillip Boutte Jr. created this concept for Mikhail, played by Alex Ferns. Mikhail was the one character to wear the suit with full gusto and gadgetry.
OPPOSITE Designed by Jared Krichevsky, these concept illustrations show a general suit design for humans to wear in Hollow Earth. After the copper-colored, sci-fi-themed suits seen in *Godzilla vs. Kong*, Adam Wingard wanted to prune that approach back and incorporate silver into the clothing. "In the last film, it made sense that they had these space suits, because they didn't really know exactly what to expect in Hollow Earth," says Wingard. "This time around, Monarch knows what to expect from the jungle environment in Hollow Earth. They know the conditions are compatible with the surface, so we moved away from the overly sci-fi look and landed on something that felt a little bit more grounded." The design went through many versions, the tabbed panel over the sleeve head being one of the only features to remain.

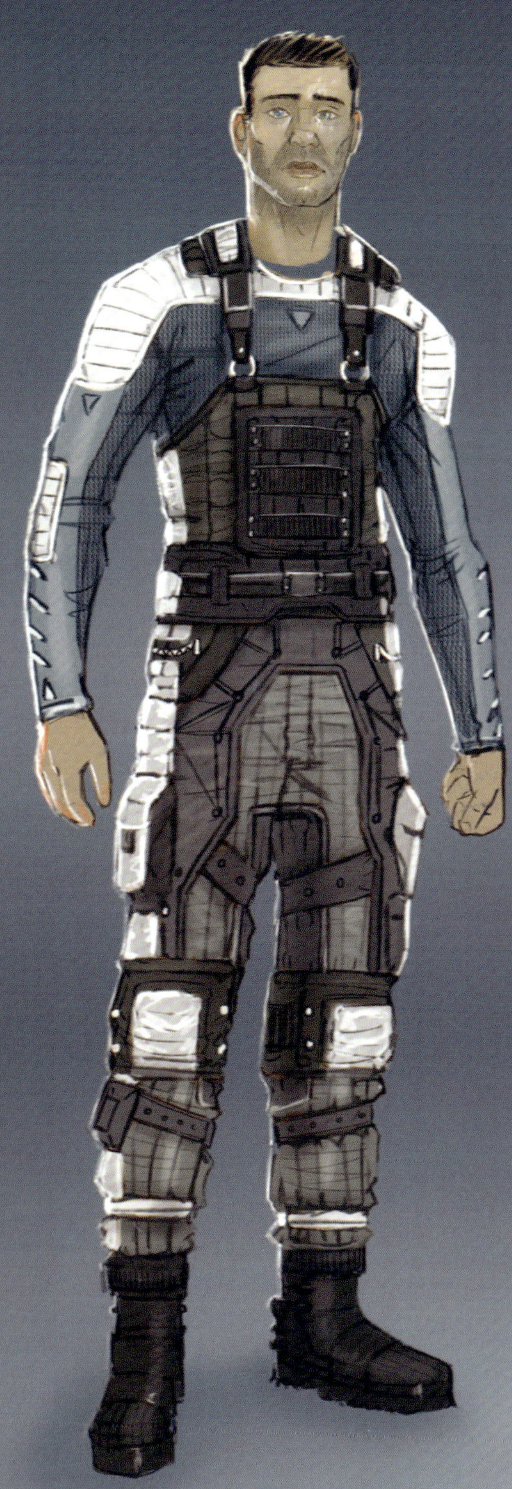

Under Suit

Jacket Vest

Combination

IWI QUEEN

THIS PAGE Three illustrations by Imogene Chayes showing the Iwi Queen's formal gowns. Adam Wingard was keen for the character to wear something that made her look like a leader, while avoiding a pampered appearance that elevated her above the other Iwi characters. **OPPOSITE** "Initially, I wanted to do something where the queen emerged in this costume that almost made her silhouette look like a creature," says Adam Wingard. The dress itself was sculptural. Susie Booth created a fabric out of pintucked silk with thousands of kebab sticks stitched into it. "We juxtaposed the sculptural shoulder pieces with delicate strings of falling beads," says costume designer Emily Seresin. "This seemed to lend strength and stillness."

IWI WARRIORS

OPPOSITE AND LEFT Three concepts for Iwi warriors by Imogene Chayes and Erin Louise Cardoo. "The idea of armor was superseded by an opalescent panel indicating their role in the community. This allowed us to introduce rich coloring into the look," says costume designer Emily Seresin.

ABOVE Initially, Wingard wanted the Iwi spears to appear to have been carved out of glowing crystals, and electrical wires were installed inside them to create light. "It was a step too far," says Wingard. "It just looked a little cheesy. But the composite plastic material that they used was so cool looking that when light hit them, they glowed anyway and they looked more natural. They created quite a few of them. I have one now! Everybody wanted an Iwi spear!"

IWI CITIZENS

OPPOSITE A selection of concept illustrations for the Iwi citizens by the Wētā Workshop team and Erin Louise Cardoo. Wingard was keen to differentiate Hollow Earth's Iwi people from those seen on Skull Island in *Godzilla vs. Kong*, inverting the color scheme.

BELOW Concepts for Iwi citizens by Imogene Chayes. Evolutions of designs showing the hierarchy of the Iwi and their different roles in Iwi society as envisioned by Emily Seresin. "Flowing lines and color harmony seemed fitting for such a peaceable society."

PART IV

TECH

PART IV: TECH

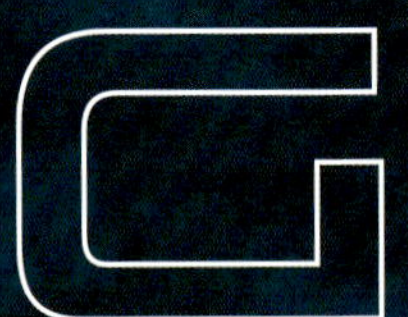

odzilla x Kong: The New Empire* is bursting with futuristic technology. With humanity taking the plunge into Hollow Earth, Monarch has developed equipment to cope with the rigors of its subterranean missions, including missile crates, surveillance cameras, sonic guns for scaring away creatures, and seismographs used to track Titan movements. "I spent a lot of time in the last movie thinking about what it is that the humans would realistically do in Hollow Earth to survive, and how they would take it to the next level now that they know what's down there," says Adam Wingard. As such, most Monarch operatives aren't outfitted with ballistic weapons, but rather with advanced gadgetry intended to distract Titans and aid in a swift escape.

Then there are Monarch's robust vehicles. Already, audiences will be familiar with the H.E.A.V. (Hollow Earth Aerial Vehicle), glimpsed in *Godzilla vs. Kong*. This antigravity craft was designed to help those traveling to Hollow Earth survive the journey's gravity inversion. For *The New Empire*, a new-and-improved vessel was created: the H.E.A.V. 2.0. "The best things that the humans can do, really, is to camouflage themselves and to blend in. And so that's where the idea [came]—of creating this vehicle that could shape-shift into colors that would scare away the Titans or give them a warning in the same way that things in nature do," says Wingard.

Equipped with the technology of biomimicry, the H.E.A.V. 2.0 emulates the vivid black-and-yellow color scheme of the flying Vertacine creatures when it arrives in Hollow Earth. Wingard took inspiration from Jean Henri Gaston Giraud, A.K.A. Moebius, the French artist who, among other endeavors, contributed designs for director Alejandro Jodorowsky's aborted attempt to adapt Frank Herbert's sci-fi epic *Dune*. "[Moebius] had a very unconventional way of creating high technology that mixes with nature," explains Wingard. "He'd have these almost garish nature patterns on huge, massive vehicles."

The craft's unique shape was influenced by the animal kingdom—specifically, fish and grasshoppers—rather than standard science fiction references. "So many spaceships now, you can kind of trace them either to a Star Wars lineage or a Marvel lineage or a Star Trek lineage," says production designer Tom Hammock. "And we wanted to do something really different."

The film's other major vessel, the M.U.L.E. (Maximum Utility Load Elevator), is Monarch's workhorse, capable of transporting huge containers. With its heavy-duty shell, it also took inspiration from Mother Nature. "The Titans always strike down. Godzilla strikes down when he knocks jets out of the air," adds Hammock. "And so we're putting all this armor at the top to protect it. But animal-wise, it was really based on a turtle, with the idea that you're protecting the cargo."

In one of *The New Empire*'s most delightfully bonkers moments, a dismantled M.U.L.E. also provides the assembled pieces for a brace fitted on Kong's arm after he's injured in a fight with Shimo. Wingard remembers talking to producer Alex Garcia: "He said essentially to me, 'You gotta come up with some sort of cool mechanical device, like a power glove thing for Kong to have.' So I was like, 'All right, if you guys are down for something that crazy!'" Dubbed "the B.E.A.S.T. (Bio Enhanced Anatomech Seismic Thunder) Glove," Kong's new gadget synced perfectly with Wingard's feelings toward the character: "I've always thought of [Kong] in the Monsterverse series as being a little bit more of an '80s action hero."

PREVIOUS PAGES The H.E.A.V. 2.0 speeds across Hollow Earth in this concept from illustrator Benjamin Donnelly.
OPPOSITE The interior of the full-scale H.E.A.V. 2.0 onstage in Australia.

4

THE H.E.A.V. 2.0

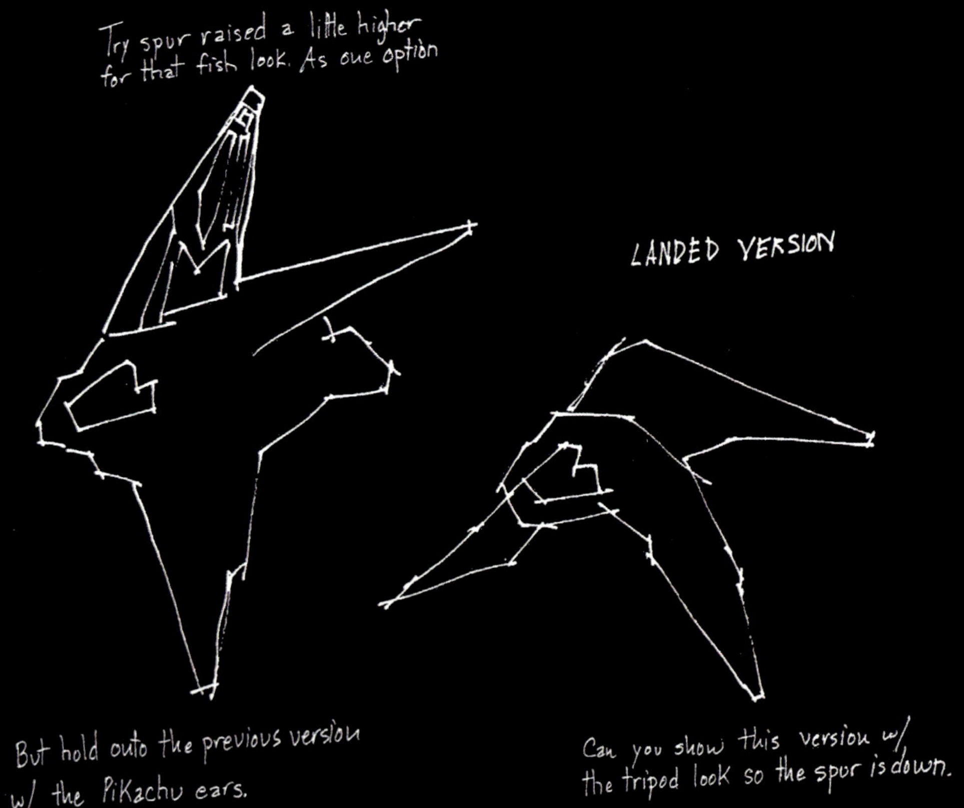

Try spur raised a little higher for that fish look. As one option
LANDED VERSION
But hold onto the previous version w/ the PiKachu ears.
Can you show this version w/ the tripod look so the spur is down.

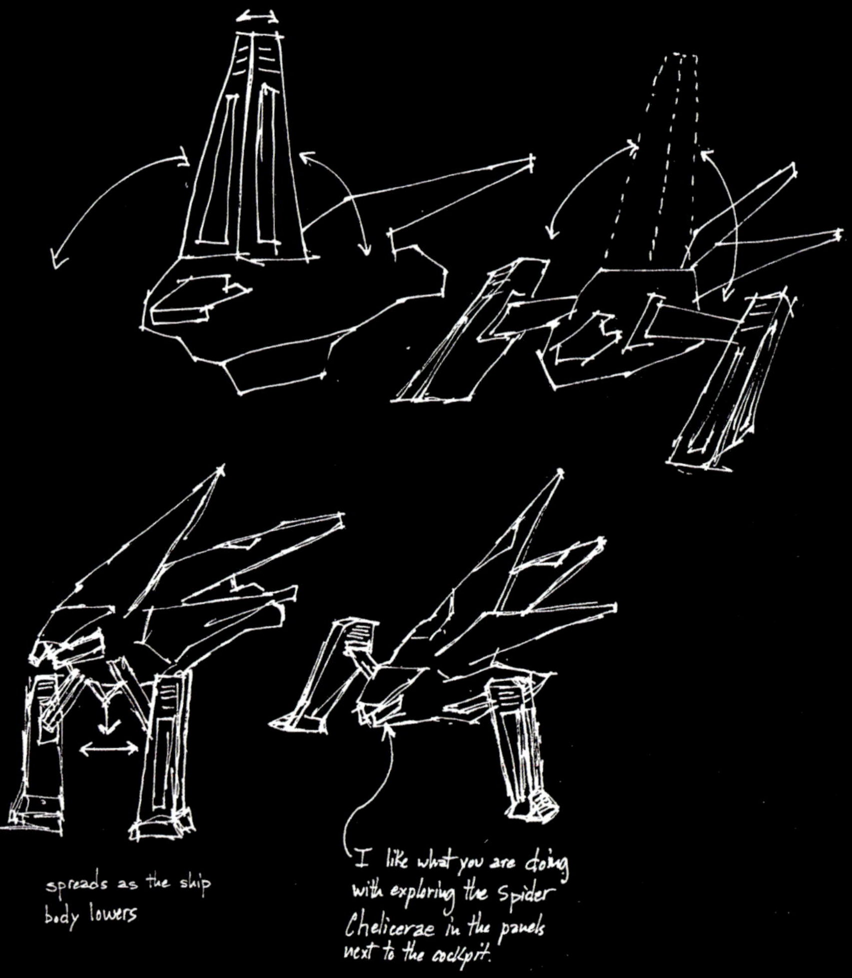

spreads as the ship body lowers
I like what you are doing with exploring the Spider Chelicerae in the panels next to the cockpit.

Look at a cluster of vertical fins like tripod fish or flying fish
Our engines fold together vertically underneath like tripod fish
Colorful vapor can look like trailing fins of fighting fish
BASIC FORM FOR NEW HEAV

Connection to Ship Body
Engine
Swap. Make Engine side wide and connection side narrow.
Landing Gear
LOOK AT GRASSHOPPER LEGS FOR LANDING GEAR ENGINE COMBO

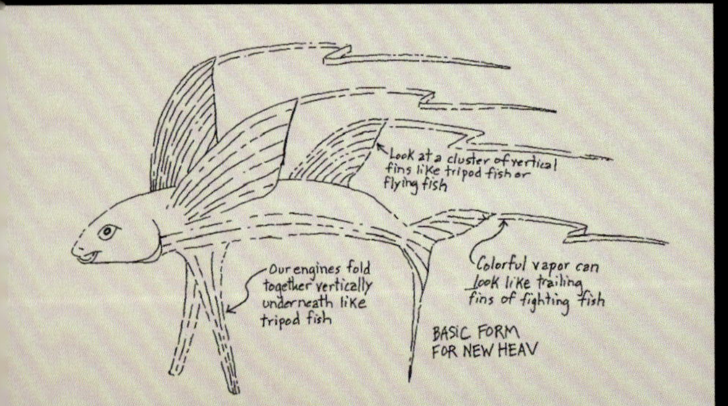

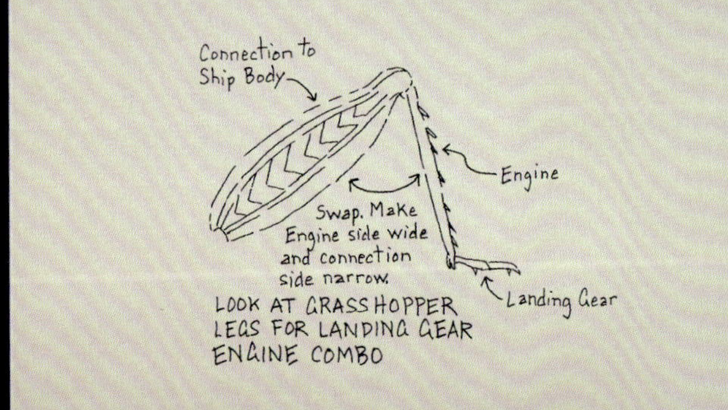

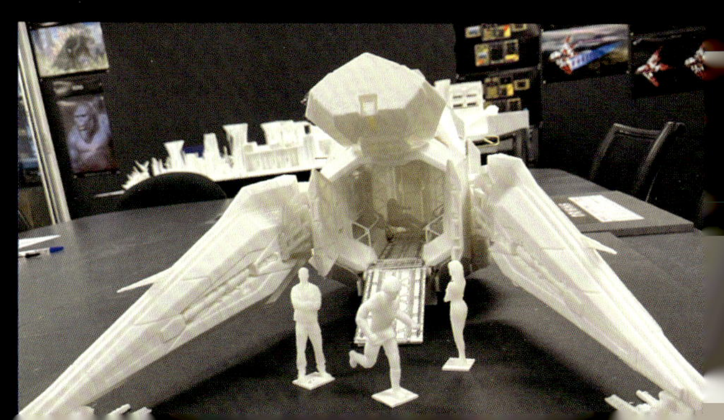

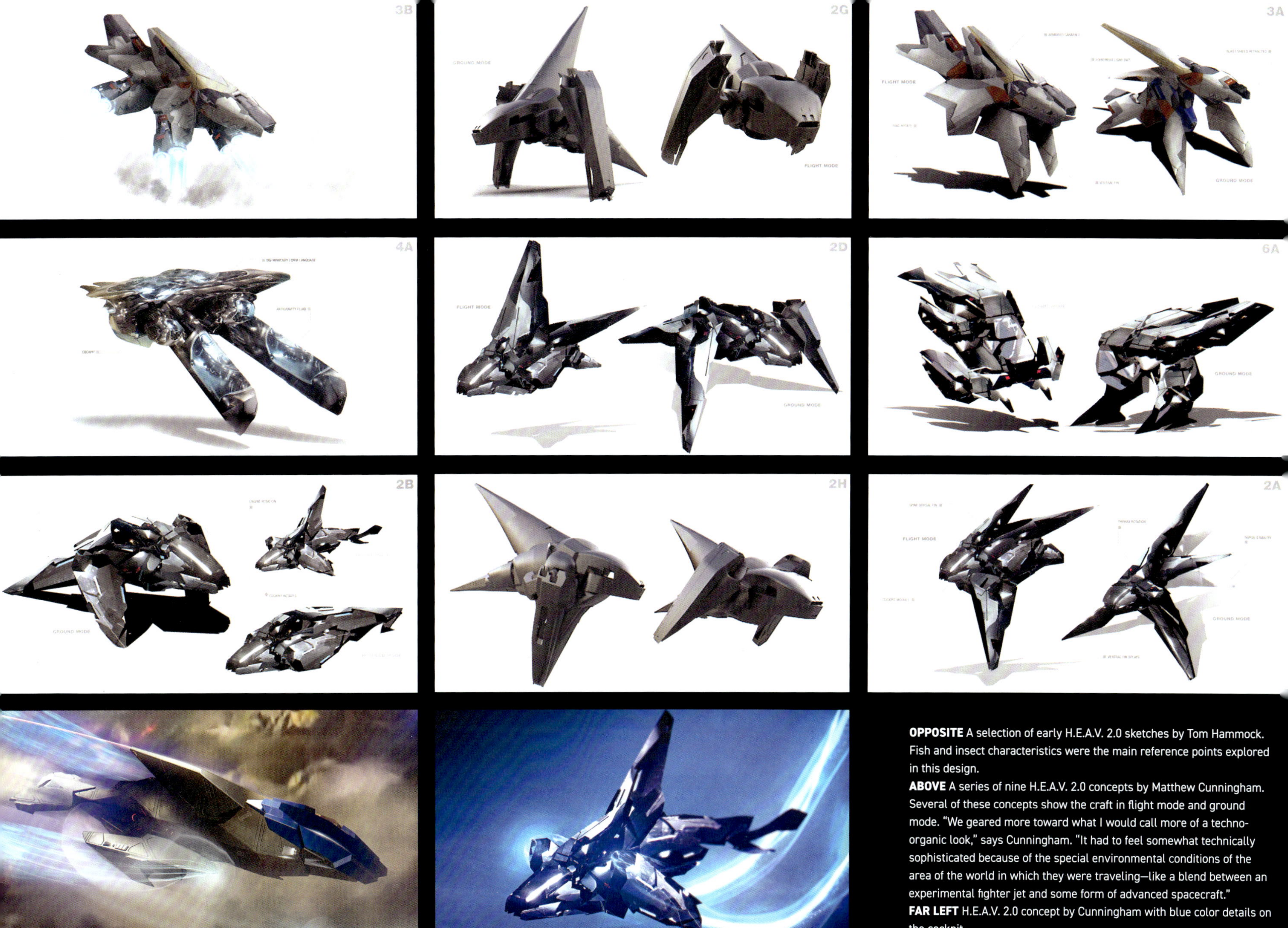

OPPOSITE A selection of early H.E.A.V. 2.0 sketches by Tom Hammock. Fish and insect characteristics were the main reference points explored in this design.

ABOVE A series of nine H.E.A.V. 2.0 concepts by Matthew Cunningham. Several of these concepts show the craft in flight mode and ground mode. "We geared more toward what I would call more of a techno-organic look," says Cunningham. "It had to feel somewhat technically sophisticated because of the special environmental conditions of the area of the world in which they were traveling—like a blend between an experimental fighter jet and some form of advanced spacecraft."

FAR LEFT H.E.A.V. 2.0 concept by Cunningham with blue color details on the cockpit.

LEFT A [illegible]arklike interpretation of the H.E.A.V. by Cun[illegible]ingham

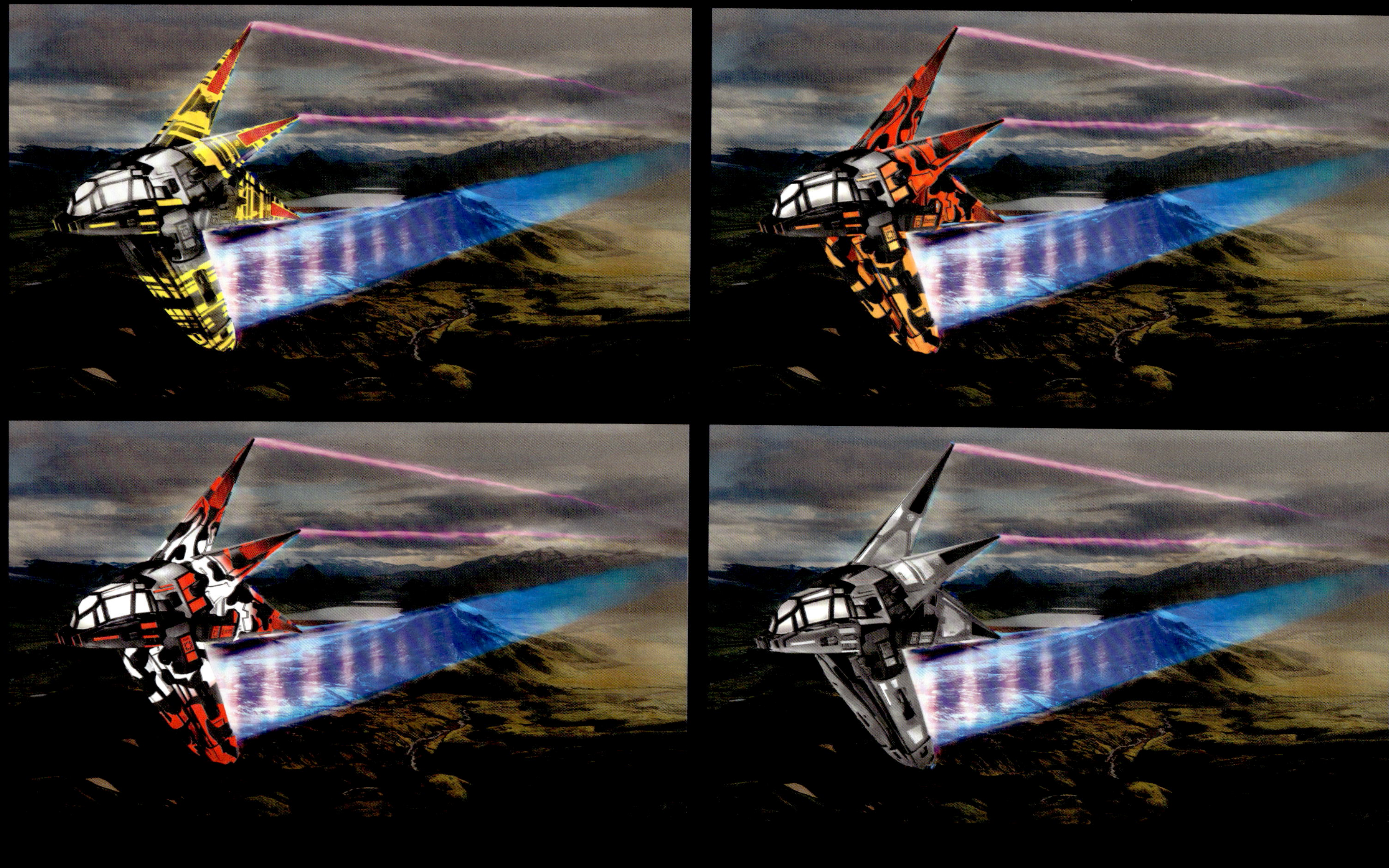

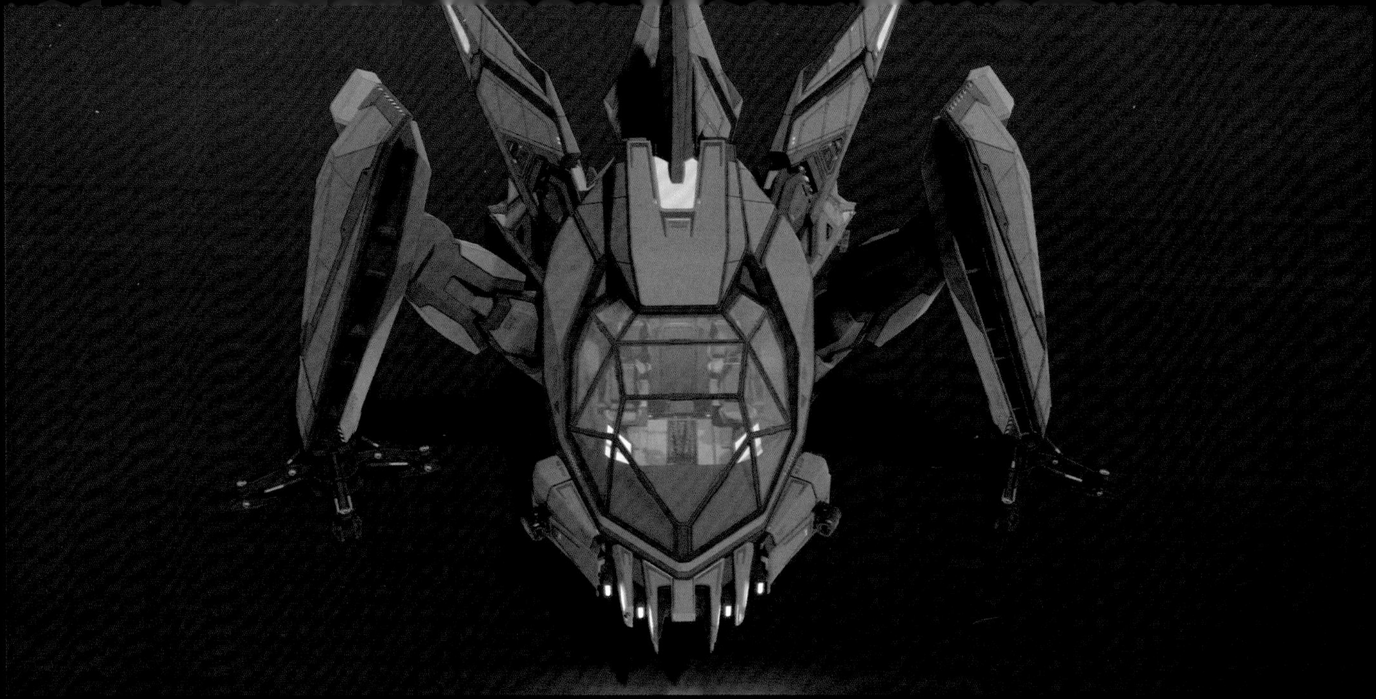

OPPOSITE Varied color schemes for the H.E.A.V. 2.0 were implemented by graphics designer Kristopher Gifford, who took inspiration from bumblebees and salamanders.

THIS PAGE A profile view of Matthew Cummingham's H.E.A.V. 2.0 design in the base color scheme, illustrated by Gifford.

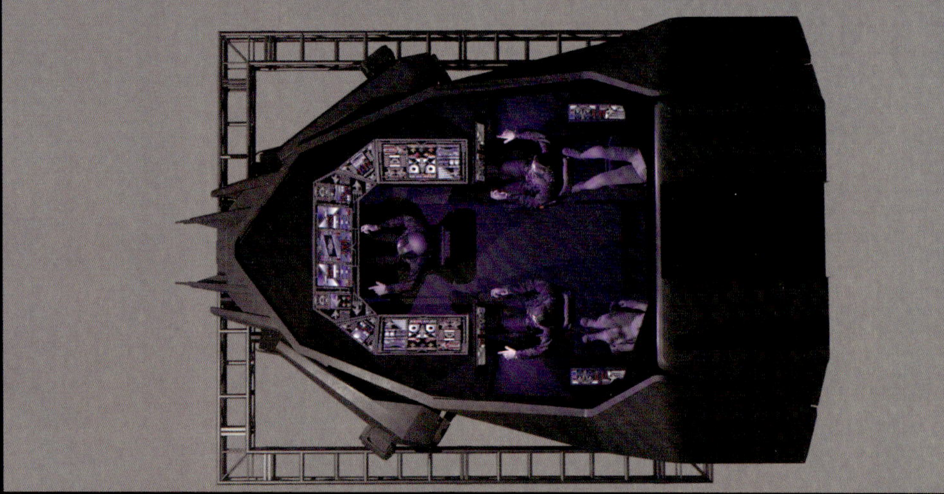

THIS PAGE A series of concepts for the H.E.A.V. 2.0 console by Benjamin Donnelly and Kristopher Gifford (above right). "Adam [Wingard] was asking for something that [looked] structurally substantial so that it wasn't just a bunch of see-through flat panels," says artist Matthew R. Cunningham. "Definitely more of a robust hardware approach."

OPPOSITE TOP LEFT "These are all sound weapons, which could, again, deter huge monsters in Hollow Earth," says Donnelly.
OPPOSITE TOP RIGHT Console concept by Michael Meyers exploring a single continuous screen.
OPPOSITE CENTER RIGHT Pilot seat concept by Donnelly.
OPPOSITE BOTTOM RIGHT Visualization of the cockpit frame by Cunningham.

OPPOSITE BOTTOM LEFT The interior cargo bay of the H.E.A.V. 2.0, courtesy of Donnelly. The door leads to the cockpit, while the space has room for four passengers, a weapon rack, pelican cases, and perimeter protective gear, used to keep insects and animals away in Hollow Earth using distractions like light, smoke, and sound.

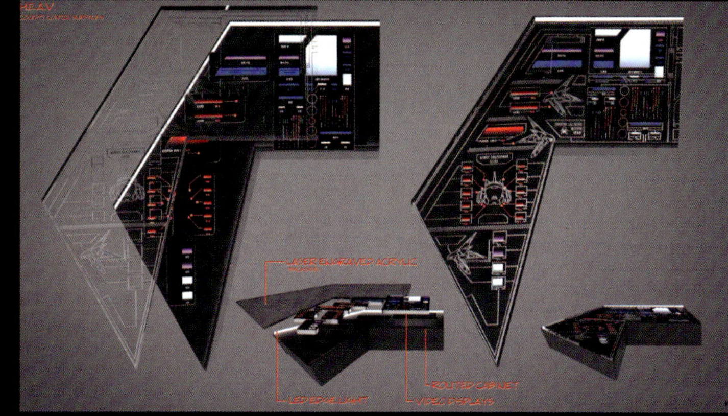
LASER ENGRAVED ACRYLIC
LED EDGE LIGHT
VIDEO DISPLAYS
ROUTED CABINET

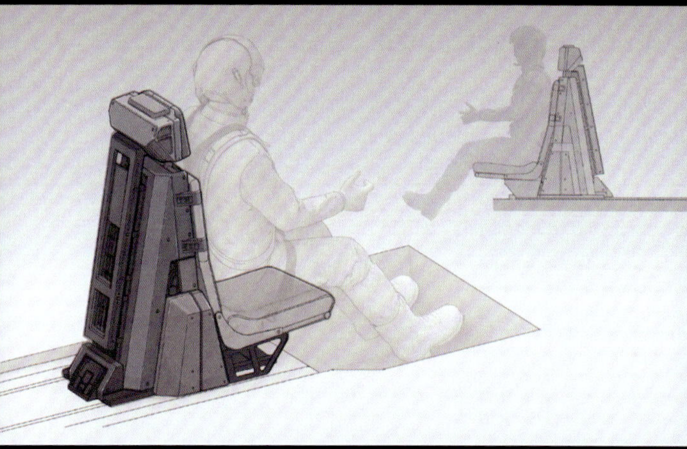

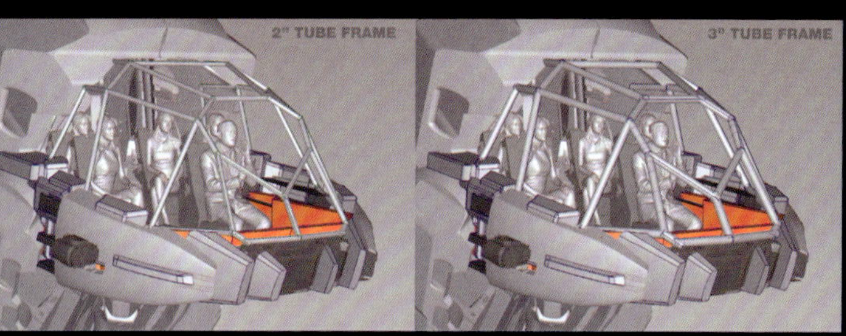
2" TUBE FRAME
3" TUBE FRAME

H.E.A.V. 2.0
BLUEPRINTS

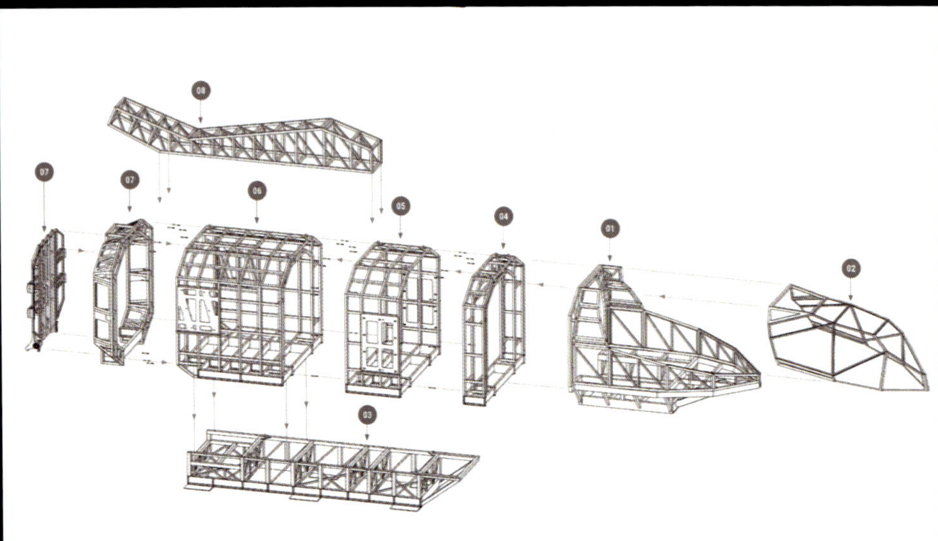

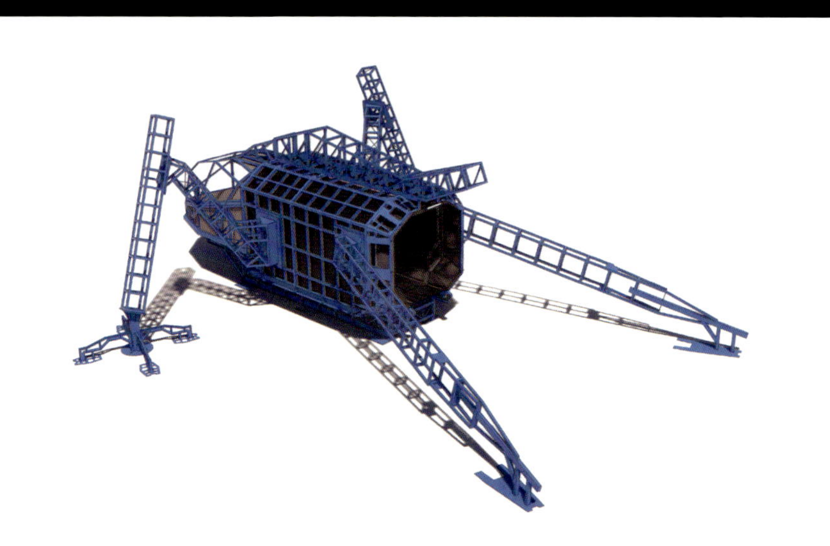

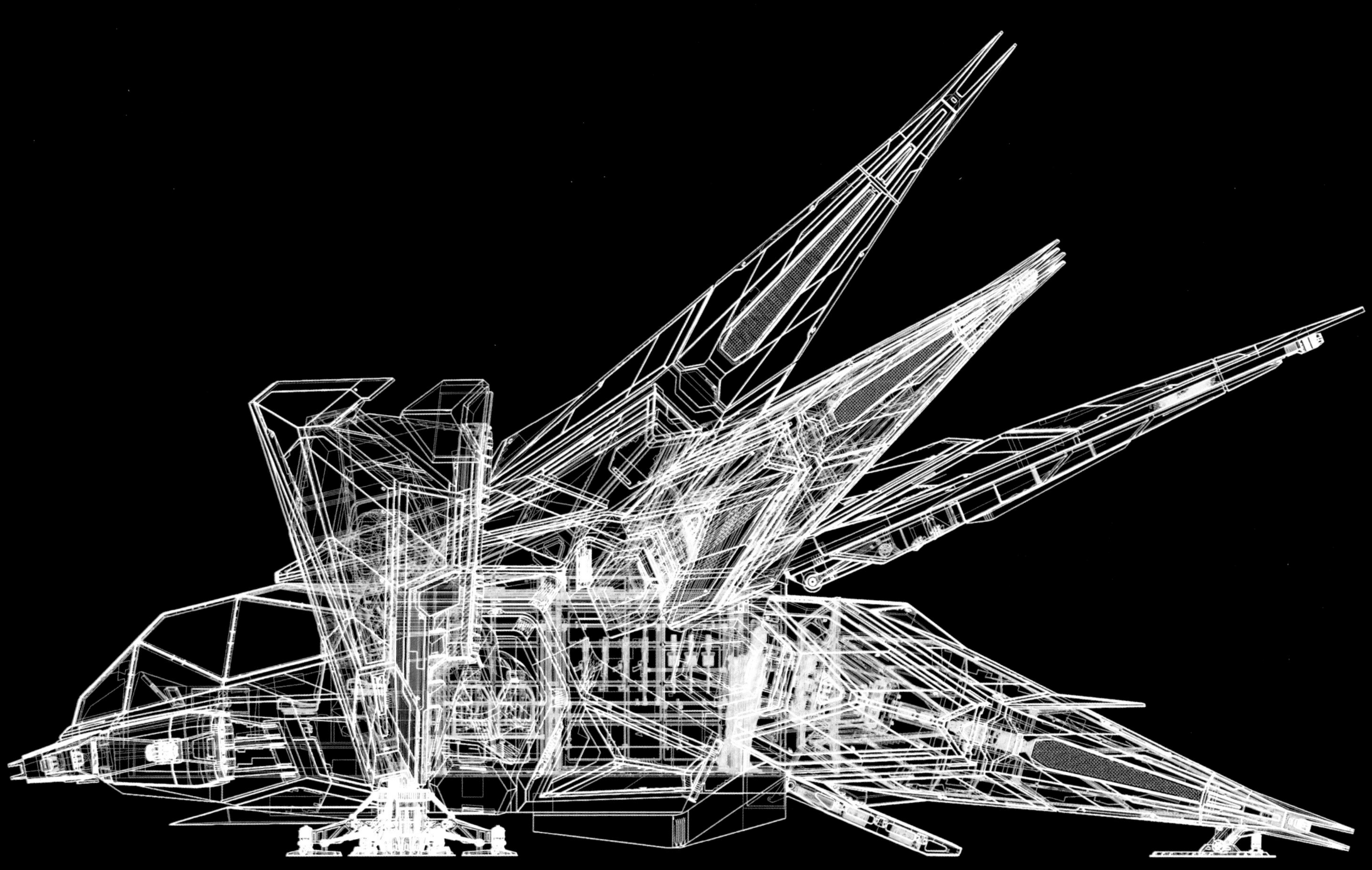

THESE PAGES Layered construction documents showing the complex steel skeleton of the H.E.A.V. 2.0 required for the ship to be viable in a variety of environments for in-camera shooting. The ship, with a total weight of 9.6 tons, came apart into fourteen pieces, which allowed for it to be moved by crane deep into jungle locations and then reassembled.

LEFT A view of the extensive carpentry required to construct the full-scale H.E.A.V. 2.0. To the far left of the image, the internal steel frame and wiring is exposed. A complex wooden framework is fitted to the steel followed by textured wooden panels, forming the surface. The final step, visible at the far right of the image, is the painted panels.

OPPOSITE LEFT COLUMN At Village Roadshow Studios, on Australia's Gold Coast, the H.E.A.V. 2.0 is under construction.

OPPOSITE TOP CENTER A view of the ramp that leads into the H.E.A.V. 2.0.

OPPOSITE TOP RIGHT The H.E.A.V. 2.0 cockpit is mounted in front of a wall of LED screens, commonly known as The Volume. Digital backgrounds can be displayed on the screens, creating a realistic environment for actors, as well as providing authentic lighting for a scene.

OPPOSITE BOTTOM RIGHT The fully assembled H.E.A.V. 2.0 weighed 9.6 tons. Here, it is seen on the set of the pyramid square, a sacred Iwi site in the village of Malenka.

Ceiling Left
1280 x 960

THE M.U.L.E.

THIS PAGE A series of M.U.L.E. concepts by Michael Meyers. Conceived as a vehicle to carry heavy loads, the M.U.L.E. can be seen carrying a shipping container in the illustrations on the opposite page.

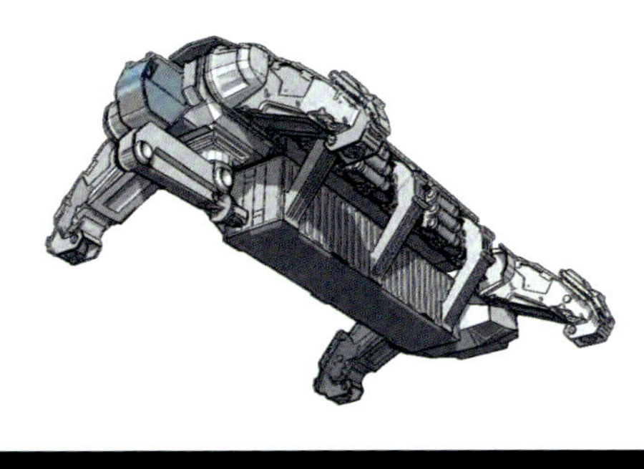

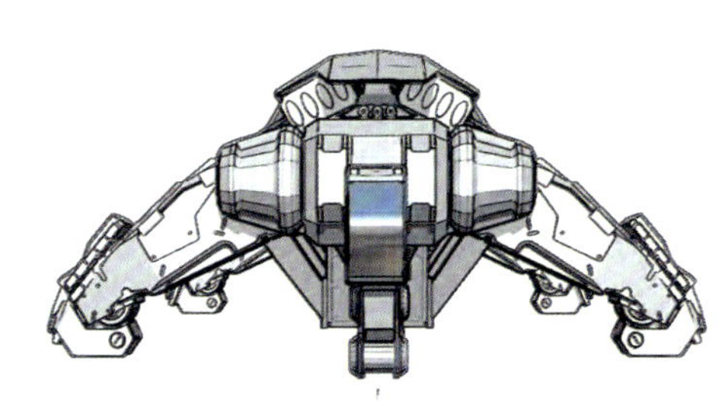

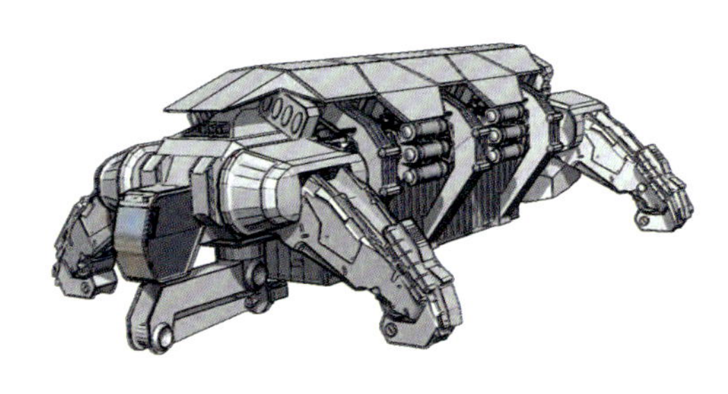

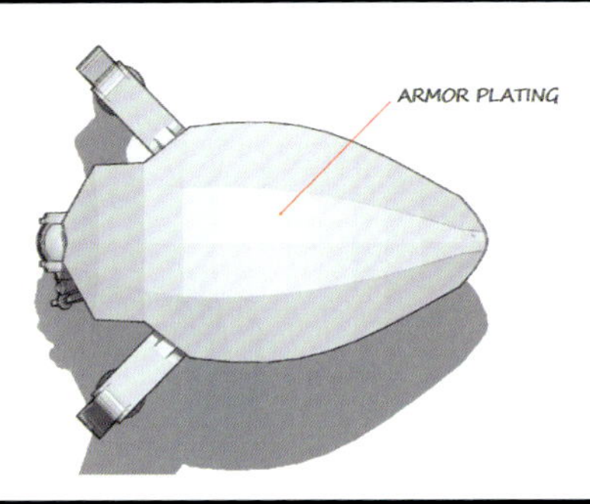

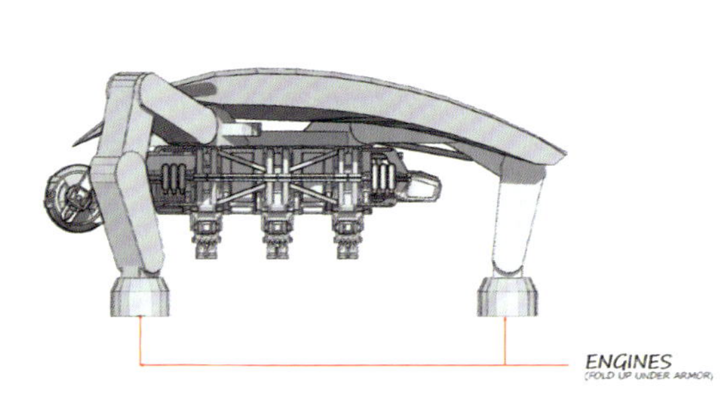

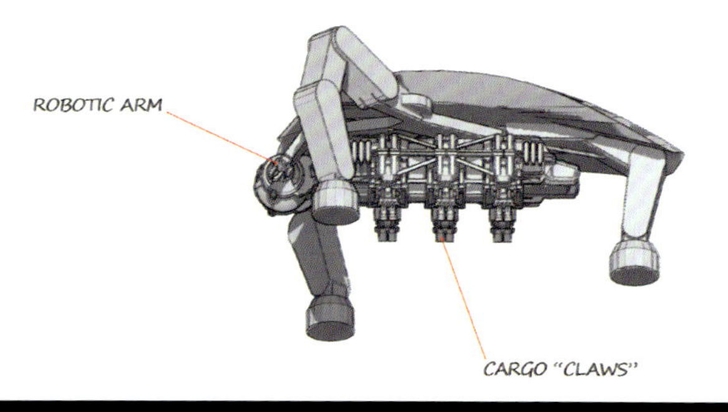

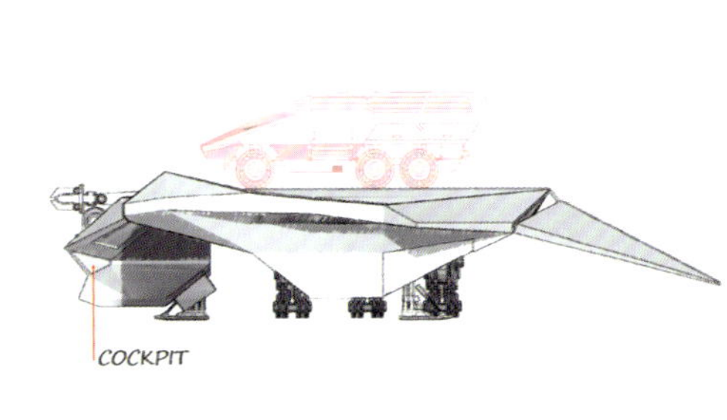

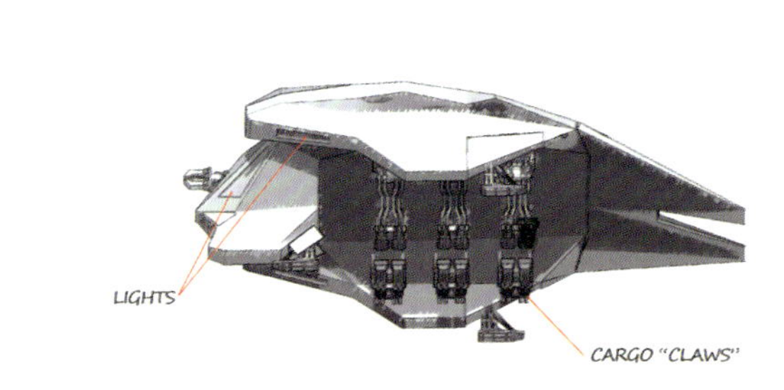

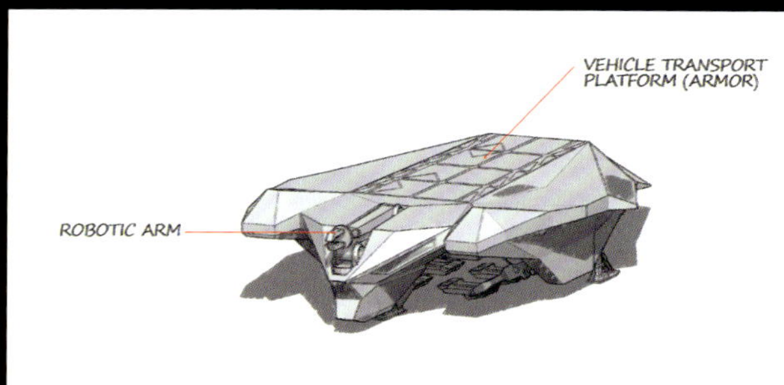

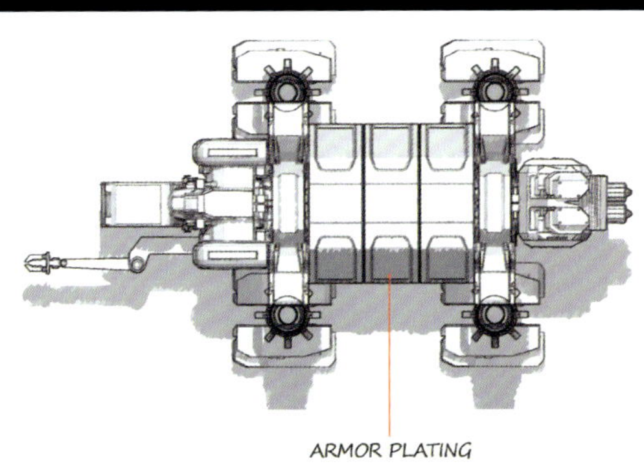

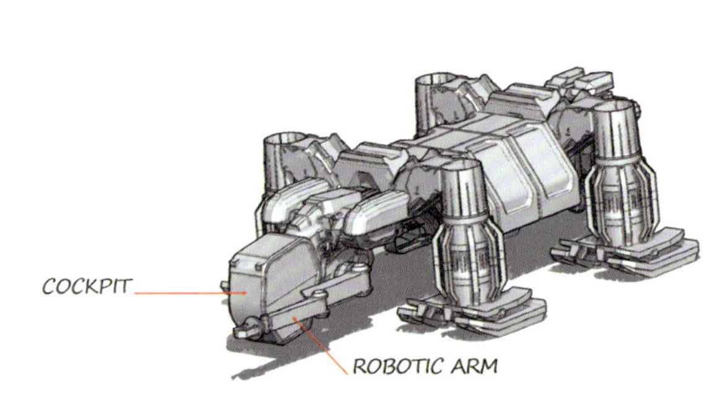

ABOVE A series of eleven early M.U.L.E. concepts by Meyers, exploring turtle and insectoid shapes. "We were looking at designs which were armored at the top to protect the cargo from Titan blows, which would come from above. We were looking to make the bulldozers or construction equipment of Hollow Earth," says Meyers.

LEFT The final design of the Maximum Utility Lift Elevator, or M.U.L.E., coined by Michael Meyers. In *The New Empire*, the M.U.L.E. is deployed to perform an impromptu dental procedure on Kong, who has an infected tooth. In Meyers's illustration, the M.U.L.E. is complete with a front-end cockpit, robotic arms, and canisters with gas repellent fitted to the sides.

BELOW LEFT "The legs [of the M.U.L.E.] are the thrusters. So, it has a lifting mode, and then it has practical thrusters in the back that make it go forward and backward," says Meyers.

BELOW CENTER The underside of the M.U.L.E., depicted by Meyers, featuring red clamps to grasp onto shipping containers and other heavy loads. Also pictured is the steel cable winch that aids in Kong's tooth extraction.

BELOW RIGHT The M.U.L.E. hovers over Kong in preparation for his unique dental surgery in this early sketch by Meyers, designed to show the scale of the Titan next to the craft.

OPPOSITE A digital rendering of the M.U.L.E. cockpit.

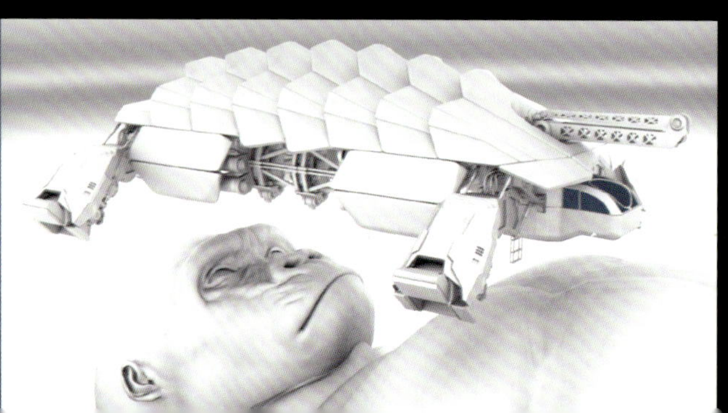

THESE PAGES A trio of designs for the cockpit of the M.U.L.E., courtesy of Michael Meyers. The construction-equipment aesthetic is still prominent, even in this advanced craft.

USE HANDLE TO
OPEN DOOR
09
07

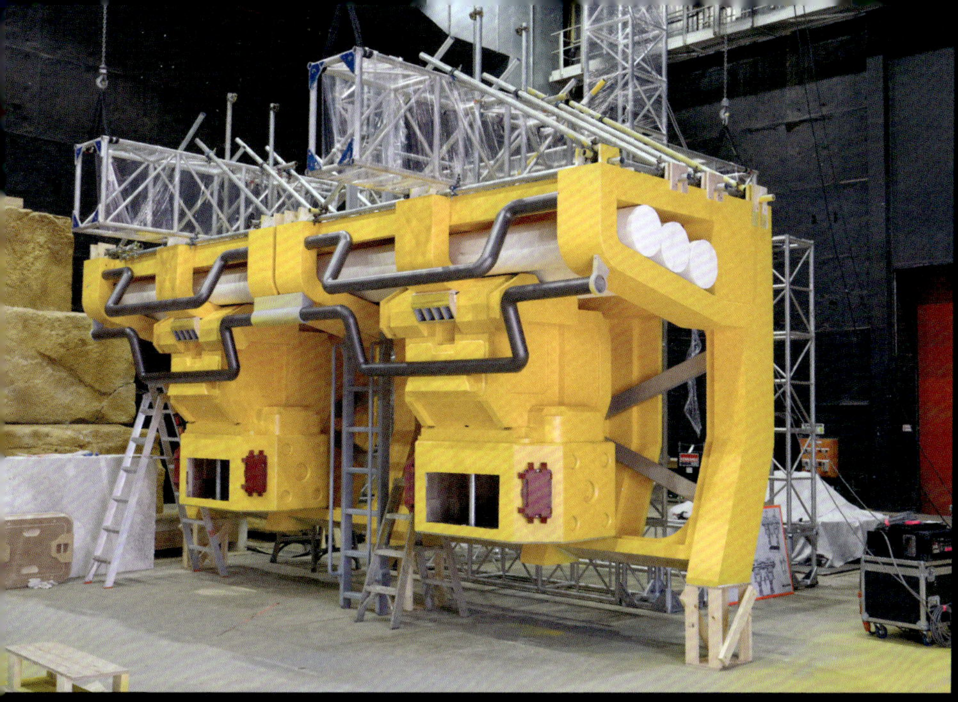

OPPOSITE PAGE AND TOP LEFT A portion of the M.U.L.E. was built on a soundstage at Village Roadshow Studios. It was used to film the tooth-extraction scene.
TOP RIGHT A miniature of a portion of the M.U.L.E.. The underbelly clamps, cable winch and pilot can be seen.
BOTTOM ROW A full-scale cockpit was also built, pictured here.

THESE PAGES After surfacing from Hollow Earth, Kong shows Jia his infected tooth in this piece by Manuel Plank-Jorge.

LEFT "In 2014, I was eating a piece of pizza, and the crust was really hard and literally cracked my tooth. [I] ended up grinding it in my sleep and the tooth actually broke off. It was a terrible experience. My worst nightmare for something like that to happen," says Adam Wingard. "And so when it came time to develop this movie, that was another one of the set pieces that I'd had in mind from the very beginning. I knew I wanted to see dental surgery on a three-hundred-foot scale!" To turn the idea of Kong's tooth extraction into reality, concept illustrator Michael Meyers was inspired by equipment found on oil rigs—a collar that can be positioned around a drill head to help move it. As seen in this illustration by Dean Sheriff, it can be wrapped around the Titan's tooth before being tightened.

TOP Kong's tooth on a soundstage, ready to be extracted.

ABOVE The full-scale build of the tooth extractor.

RIGHT A digital version of the winch hook.

THE B.E.A.S.T. GLOVE

THIS PAGE This illustration of Kong wearing the B.E.A.S.T. Glove is by Michael Meyers. "There [were] a lot of issues to solve in terms of how they get [the glove] on his arm, how it would stay on his arm, and what it would be made from," says Meyers. "I came up with the idea of taking apart a couple of M.U.L.E.s and repurposing them. The loops on his fingers are the landing gear from the M.U.L.E. And then everything else on this is a piece of two M.U.L.E.s that have been cut apart and welded back together to make the glove."
OPPOSITE LEFT A 3-D turnaround of Kong's glove.
OPPOSITE RIGHT Three early designs for the glove by Meyers show its intricate design, including armor plating and a gas charging unit.

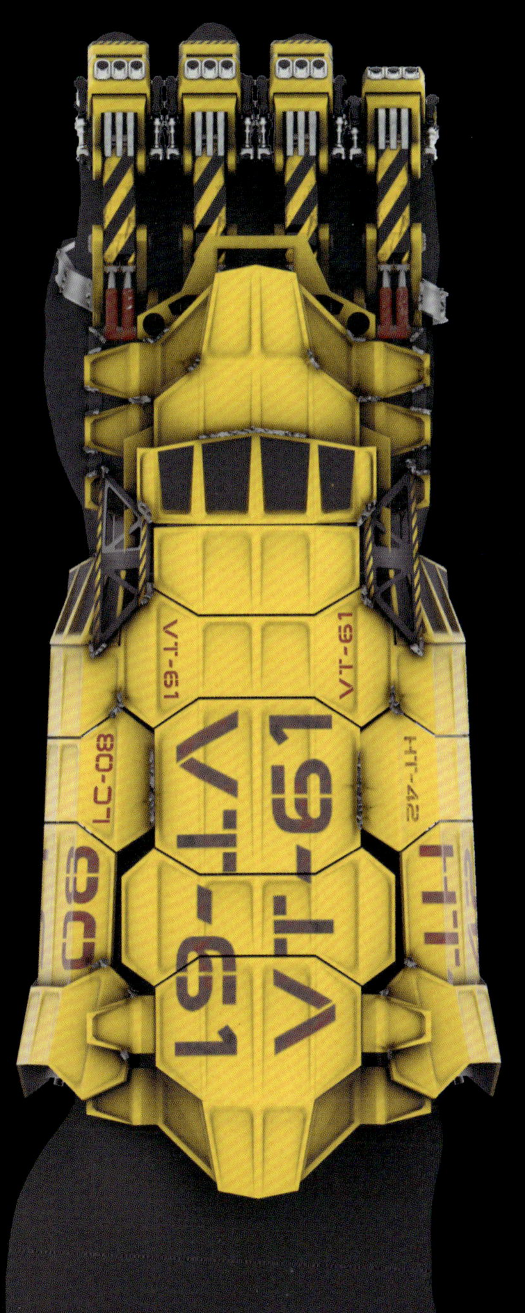

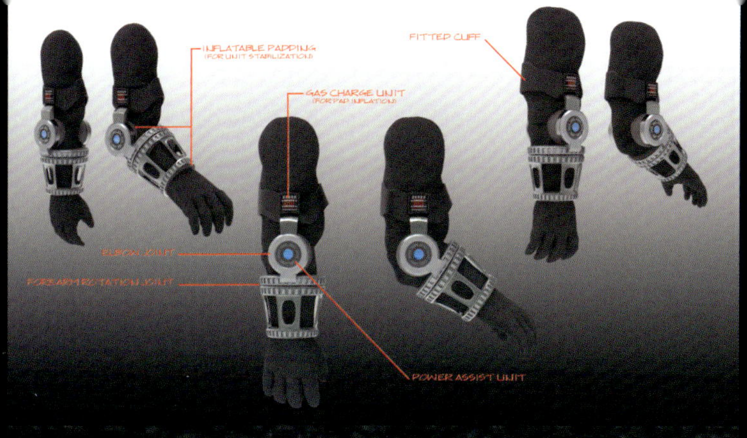
INFLATABLE PADDING
(FOR UNIT STABILIZATION)
FITTED CUFF
GAS CHARGE UNIT
(FOR PAD INFLATION)
ELBOW JOINT
FOREARM ROTATION JOINT
POWER ASSIST UNIT

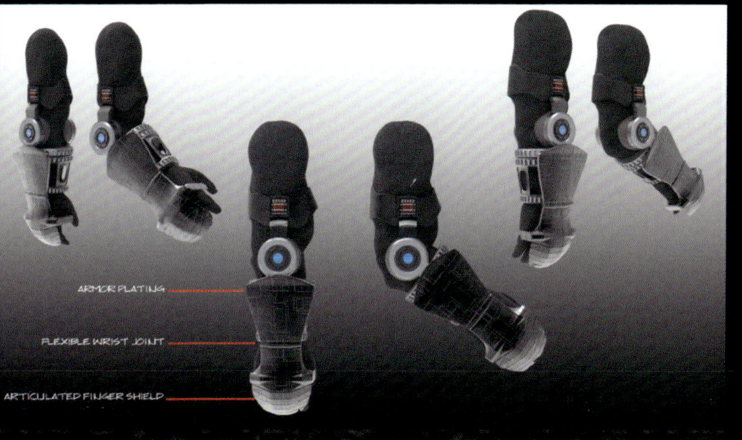
ARMOR PLATING
FLEXIBLE WRIST JOINT
ARTICULATED FINGER SHIELD

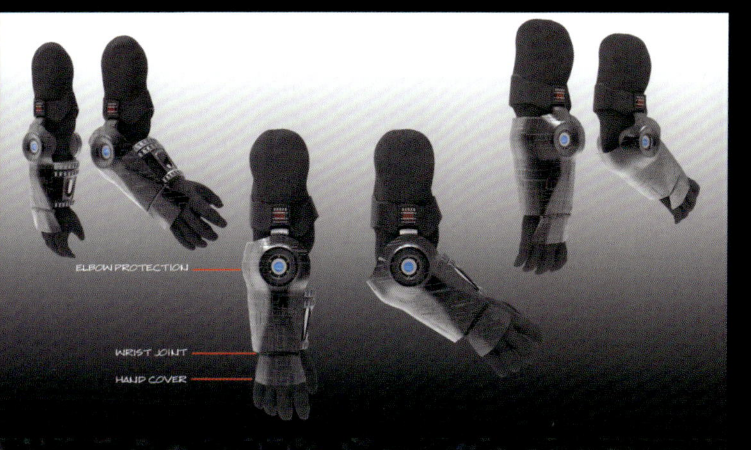
ELBOW PROTECTION
WRIST JOINT
HAND COVER

PART
V

THE SURFACE WORLD

PART V:

THE SURFACE WORLD

In the early scenes of *Godzilla x Kong: The New Empire*, audiences are introduced to new parts of the Earth's surface not yet seen in the Monsterverse. To begin with, Godzilla is found in the eternal city of Rome, where he discovers the perfect place to recuperate after defeating fellow Titan Scylla. "After *King of the Monsters*, his [lair] has been destroyed," says Adam Wingard. "So I thought, 'Well, where does he go?'" The answer was Rome's ancient battleground, the Colosseum.

In the initial development, the Hard Rock Stadium in Miami Gardens, the home of the NFL's Miami Dolphins, was considered as a suitable resting place. The idea was soon rejected, however. "Miami's stadium is square, and it didn't seem comfortable for Godzilla," says production designer Tom Hammock. "And so, eventually, we asked, 'If Godzilla was going to take a catnap, where would he take it?' The Colosseum is one of the most iconic things on the planet. And so we ended up there."

When Godzilla departs Rome, he eventually finds himself on a collision course with another Titan, the dragon-like creature Tiamat. Entering her watery lair deep in the Arctic Ocean, Godzilla kills Tiamat and steals reserves of energy stored there. The energy causes a metamorphosis in Godzilla's appearance, and he evolves into a more battle-ready Titan. Wingard points out that it's an unusual choice by Godzilla, who will normally let other Titans be if they're not encroaching on his territory. But here, Tiamat's energy was required to help Godzilla prepare for the fights to come.

"It's kind of unique in this movie where Godzilla is almost selfish," says Wingard. "Tiamat is minding her own business in her own territory, off to the side—kind of an agreed truce. And Godzilla's, like, 'OK, we got a real problem here, I'm gonna have to kick you out of your home.' And he eviscerates her. So it's kind of an interesting character thing, because it shows that Godzilla is going to do whatever it takes to protect the Earth, even if it means killing a somewhat innocent Titan. So, R.I.P., Tiamat!"

The film also introduces the Monarch base in Barbados, where a Vile Vortex leads to Hollow Earth. The Caribbean island was in stark contrast to Antarctica, where a vortex was first seen in *Godzilla vs. Kong*. "We didn't want to go back to Antarctica, necessarily, for the portal to Hollow Earth," says Wingard. "We felt like Monarch is probably discovering all these new portals all over the world." For Wingard, the choice perfectly tapped into the bright, eye-popping color scheme he wanted. "This pristine, tropical Barbados environment—we knew it would reflect this beautiful color palette in a nice way."

The design for the Barbados base also served a narrative purpose: The concrete structure is painted with yellow-and-black chevrons and the vortex pillars are decorated in red-and-white checks, which are meant to offer visual cues for any approaching Titans.

"Within nature, there are two universal color schemes that say, 'Don't touch me,'" explains Hammock. "One is yellow and black. One is red and white. Those are ways that nature says, 'Don't touch,' and it's these color combinations. Monarch's design plan is similar to how it works for poison dart frogs or bumblebees . . . Instead of trying to camouflage their bases, Monarch is making them incredibly colorful in these universal color combinations so that Titans know to not touch them, to protect themselves." As Wingard notes, it's one of his production designer's great skills. "Tom's always thinking about the functionality. Whenever he's designing these outlandish sets, he's trying to think of it in a true functional way, even if this is a completely fantastical environment."

PREVIOUS PAGES A close-up of the Barbados Monarch facility by Manuel Plank-Jorge, with figures to show scale. This base features bright color schemes similar to those of the H.E.A.V., a visual warning to Titans to stay away.
OPPOSITE An aerial view of the Monarch base and the Vile Vortex entrance, depicted here by Manuel Plank-Jorge.

LEFT In this concept piece by Ben Wootten, Godzilla curls up inside the Colosseum.

ABOVE "I was just looking at my cat, Mischief, in her cat bed," says Adam Wingard. "And I thought, 'Well, what if this was the Roman Colosseum? In the way that Mischief was laying in it, that could be Godzilla.'"

RIGHT Storyboards by Micah Brenner show Godzilla in Rome's Colosseum before he awakens and leaves a trail of destruction behind him.

GODZILLA AWAKENS

OPPOSITE PAGE Storyboards by Micah Brenner show Godzilla trouncing Scylla and then lying down inside the Roman Colosseum.
THIS PAGE A group of tourists takes a selfie with the hibernating Godzilla moments before the Titan awakens. "Godzilla's regarding them before he moves . . . there's a nice level of intelligence there," says illustrator Ben Wootten.

evolution

THESE PAGES In the Arctic Ocean, a submarine comes across an eerie Godzilla-like shape, here depicted by Manuel Plank-Jorge, hidden behind a wall of ice, only to discover Godzilla has shed his skin after killing Tiamat and absorbing her reserves of energy. "I was looking at shed snakeskin for reference. And I was thinking, How do you illuminate this? You're so deep down in the ocean, and of course, everything's black. You should be able to somehow recognize Godzilla, but at the same time, you shouldn't. And so it should be somehow mysterious, but just revealing enough that you kind of understand where this could go," says Plank-Jorge.

Jared Krichevsky showing the

Prominent Face & Body Spikes
Translucent Barbed Dorsal Spikes
Broader Shoulders
Greener Hue, Fresh From Molting
Longer Arms
Stomach Tucked In
Longer, Thinner Legs
Old
Evolved

OPPOSITE This piece by Jared Krichevsky illustrates the differences between Godzilla's initial form and his evolved self.
LEFT TOP AND BOTTOM Maquette of the evolved Godzilla by Krichevsky.

THESE PAGES A concept illustration by Jared Krichevsky shows Godzilla, now in his evolved form, causing carnage in an urban setting. "Godzilla molts in the ice and sheds his skin to prepare to battle Shimo. And from there, there are subtle changes," says Tom Hammock. "He gets his elbow spikes, he gets some spines to protect his eyes around the face. Because his skin is new, like a reptile or a spider when they shed their skin, he's a little brighter. He's a touch more green and the fins on his back are a little more pink/purple when they light up because his skin isn't totally hardened yet, so you can see the veins."

TIAMAT

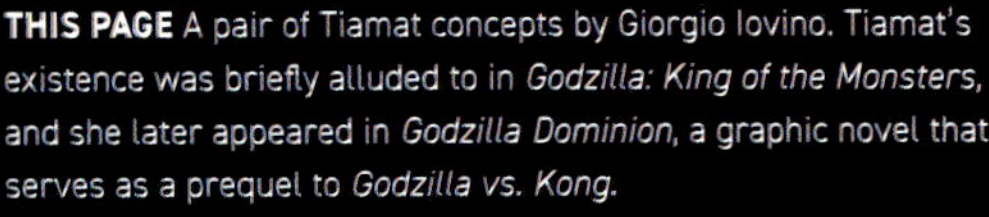

THIS PAGE A pair of Tiamat concepts by Giorgio Iovino. Tiamat's existence was briefly alluded to in *Godzilla: King of the Monsters*, and she later appeared in *Godzilla Dominion*, a graphic novel that serves as a prequel to *Godzilla vs. Kong*.
OPPOSITE These Tiamat concepts by Joe Lucchese show two colorways for the serpentlike Titan.

THE MONARCH BASE

PREVIOUS PAGES

PAGE 122 An overview map of the Barbados-based Monarch facility.

PAGE 123 TOP In this illustration by Manuel Plank-Jorge, red-and-white towers plunge into the water to create a vortex that leads to Hollow Earth.

PAGE 123 BOTTOM LEFT An overhead view of Monarch's Barbados facility.

PAGE 123 BOTTOM RIGHT H.E.A.V.s and M.U.L.E.s can be seen in this concept illustration of the Monarch facility by Plank-Jorge.

THIS PAGE TOP A Monarch missile crate illustrated by Alex Moy.

THIS PAGE BOTTOM Introduced in *Godzilla: King of the Monsters*, the Orca device is used for extremely rudimentary communication with the Titans. This is a concept for a miniaturized Titan-tracking device by Michael Meyers.

OPPOSITE This concept piece by Moy shows a look at the interior of a command center within Monarch's Barbados facility.

MF FILTRATE
MF CIP
MF FILTRATE
MF CIP
MF FEED WATER

PART VI

JOURNEY
INTO THE HOLLOW
EARTH

PART VI:
JOURNEY INTO THE HOLLOW EARTH

Hollow Earth—the land of the Titans—is a world filled with terror, despite its mesmeric beauty, created through a cunning mix of VFX and real-world footage. "We wanted it to be deceptive in its own way," says Wingard. "It's one of the prettiest-looking locations in the film, but it's filled with danger." Even Kong sets his own traps as a means for survival. The film's opening sequence sees him chased by Wart Dogs across Hollow Earth, only for some to be crushed by a rockfall he orchestrates.

Wingard was inspired by the Mesoamerican rainforest. And so I had the idea of Kong being chased to the jungle," he says. "What environments do we want to have there? And then I started thinking about the idea of putting these traps in." It was also a way, Wingard adds, to show Kong's evolution: "He's not just an ape. He's not just a monster. He can understand machinery to a certain degree."

For the humans, Hollow Earth's surprises prove fatal, as poor Mikhail discovers when a monster disguised as a tree snatches him, sealing his doom. Yet Hollow Earth is not all deadly; it's also filled with wonder, like the Iwi ruins—stone buildings, columns, and carvings half-hidden by the dense jungle foliage. To create this, production designer Tom Hammock and his team studied remains from ancient civilizations, ranging from Caral in Peru to Nan Madol in Micronesia and Angkor Wat in Cambodia. "We were just looking at the architectural language of a number of stone-based architectural traditions," says Hammock. "[We asked] ourselves, for Hollow Earth, 'How do you take that architectural order and produce a more simplistic, geometric version of it?'"

At the heart of Hollow Earth is the Iwi village of Malenka, a place of great mystery and powerful technology. Wingard compares it to Agartha, the fabled lost kingdom of the inner Earth first suggested by French philosopher and occultist Joseph Alexandre Saint-Yves in the late 1800s. Here, it is a world that defies the physics of the surface, where gravity can shift. It is also here where the Iwi signal for Godzilla by using a powerful quartz stalactite held in the Iwi ceremonial chamber as their beacon. This signal is the same vibrating call that Jia responds to, leading Andrews and the others into Hollow Earth.

With its stunning flora that glows purple in the nighttime darkness, Hollow Earth is utterly beautiful to look at. Hammock conceptualized that this plant life spread from this world and onto the surface of our planet. "There used to be this cold-climate rainforest that covered Antarctica," explains Hammock. "And that rainforest is largely extinct, but little pieces of it are left at the very base of Chile and Argentina, in Tasmania, New Zealand, and New Caledonia. So, there are little pockets of this ecosystem still left—this really unique, ancient forest that's made up of living fossils. And there's a piece of it in Northern Australia, up where it hits Papua New Guinea. It's the oldest rainforest on the entire planet."

"The raw beauty of the world's oldest tropical rainforest, the Daintree in Northern Queensland Australia, breathes life into the hidden world of Hollow Earth. Every plant, every vine, and every drop of rain adds logistical challenges that help fuel the magic. The Daintree was a reminder that in filmmaking, as in the Monsterverse, the most thrilling battles are those fought alongside nature," says Eric McLeod, producer.

With this in mind, McLeod and Wingard steered the production to shoot in the Daintree Rainforest in Queensland, Australia. Although *The New Empire* would utilize facilities at Village Roadshow Studios on Australia's Gold Coast, building the Iwi ruins and village there, the director didn't want to create Hollow Earth's jungles on a soundstage. It would take days to get to the rainforest location, with shooting taking place literally where the road north ends. "It was a big trek to get the crew there," he says. "It's very remote . . . but we knew it was worth it because it had these environments people really had never shot in before. The plants in the area that we shot, some of them are up to two thousand years old. This is a very ancient forest. And it's interesting how a place like that really does have a magical quality to it. I remember, everybody was having weird dreams when we started shooting there."

The night Wingard arrived, he dreamed that he fell and rolled over next to a tree and it started strangling him with its roots. "It was almost like the jungle had this power," he says. "And it was warning me not to mess with it. And so I really took that to heart. I was on the edge every day we were in that jungle, because when you have a lot of equipment, especially in a movie like this, you have people just knocking over stuff, ripping up things." Wingard took it upon himself to make sure everyone knew to treat the jungle with the utmost respect. "I mean, that's the kind of stuff you're looking for in these types of movies," he adds. "You're looking for that real magical influence to come in and take it to the next level."

PREVIOUS PAGES This illustration by Dean Sherriff shows a wrecked original H.E.A.V. 1.0—the aftermath of the Skar King's attack on a Monarch base in Hollow Earth. "The seed sacks hanging down . . . Tom [Hammock] wanted to put those everywhere. He wanted to have something you can actually build and that you could dress the jungle with," says Sherriff.
OPPOSITE Illustrator Michael Sheffels's concept of Malenka's mirror pyramids, which are nearly touching due to the tunnel-like environment of Hollow Earth.

THE MONITORING STATION

RIGHT In *The New Empire*, the Skar King destroys a Monarch monitoring station in Hollow Earth. Here, Tom Hammock's sketch of the scene is laid over a photo of the real-world location in Queensland.
BELOW AND BOTTOM CENTER Surveillance-camera concepts by Michael Meyers.
BOTTOM RIGHT A Monarch seismograph as envisioned by Alex Moy.
OPPOSITE In this artwork, Dean Sherriff depicts Dr. Andrews and the others searching outside Monarch's wrecked monitoring station. The Skar King's handprint can be seen on the building at the rear.

WART DOGS

THESE PAGES "I knew I wanted the movie to open up in a chase, just get right to it, and put you in Kong's perspective for five minutes straight," says Adam Wingard. "That way, the precedent has been set. You're not waiting for the Titans to show up in the film." These concepts by Matt Allsopp show two perspectives of Kong running from a pack of Wart Dogs, which serves as the opening sequence of *The New Empire*.

THESE PAGES These storyboards by Richard Bennett depict the sequence in which Kong springs a trap on the Wart Dogs. The vicious creatures are not deterred by Kong's pit trap, so he makes a brutal example of one of them.

OPPOSITE An amalgamation of wolf and warthog, the Wart Dog is Kong's first foe. This page features four designs by Jared Krichevsky. The bottom right image was used by Adam Wingard during the pre-viz phase, when sequences were mapped out in rudimentary computer form before moving onto a Wart Dog design that is more intimidating.

THIS PAGE Here, we see the evolution of the creature designed by Alex Ries. The top right image is the closest to what is ultimately seen in the film. Wingard explains, "Everybody knows Kong can take on just about anything. And so it needed to be believable that these things were, as a pack, extremely vicious and you wouldn't want them near you. And ultimately, the final version, they almost look like zombie dogs."

HITTING THE ROAD

ABOVE At the start of *The New Empire*, Kong lives alone in his Hollow Earth lair. "This illustration was a nod to the 1933 black-and-white *King Kong* movie, where Kong is high up on a ledge overlooking vast and primitive hunting grounds," says Michele Moen.

OPPOSITE This illustration by Moen shows Kong in a more cavernous concept for his lair.

ABOVE This concept illustration by Dean Sherriff shows Kong dropping his axe as he journeys through Hollow Earth. Throughout, the story depicts Kong's intelligence. "He can understand machinery to a certain degree, which we established in the last film with the axe," says Wingard. "The fact that he can utilize a weapon like an axe . . . there's more going on there."
OPPOSITE In this pair of concepts, Sherriff provides a look at Kong in a Hollow Earth cave, flanked by skeletons of the ancient Great Apes, who have long since perished. The sight of Kong's forebears leaves the Titan feeling yet more lonely.

OPPOSITE "This was a lush, green, prehistoric environment to give a sense of beauty without the danger of the red colors. Kong shows surprise at discovering Suko, and Suko is a little shy and tentative

important," says Michele Moen. In this concept, pieces of the Hollow Earth are collapsing in on itself, like the peeling of an onion.

ABOVE This concept by Moen showcases the intense red landscape

TOP In this illustration by Michele Moen, Kong and Suko can be seen traversing crystalline structures. "This was a smaller tunnel offshoot of Hollow Earth where the shape and scale were more apparent," says Moen. "Tom [Hammock] and Adam [Wingard] really liked the dramatic heaven and hell paintings of the early-1800s English Romantic painter John Martin. These paintings were to be my inspiration."

BOTTOM This illustration by Moen features Kong and Suko exchanging food in the Skar King's realm.

OPPOSITE TOP In this illustration by Moen, Kong and Suko encounter the Drownviper.

ABOVE Kong and Suko travel through Hollow Earth in this artwork by Dean Sherriff, crossing a bridge made of a fossilized spinal column that separates the Hollow Earth jungle from the Skar King's empire. **OPPOSITE** This illustration by Sherriff shows a side-on view of the bone bridge. In both images, purple sulfur can be seen pouring down from nearby rocks, inspired by the Kawah Ijen volcano in Indonesia. **FOLLOWING PAGES** In another illustration by Sherriff, Kong beckons Suko to follow him across the bone bridge.

JUNGLE RUINS

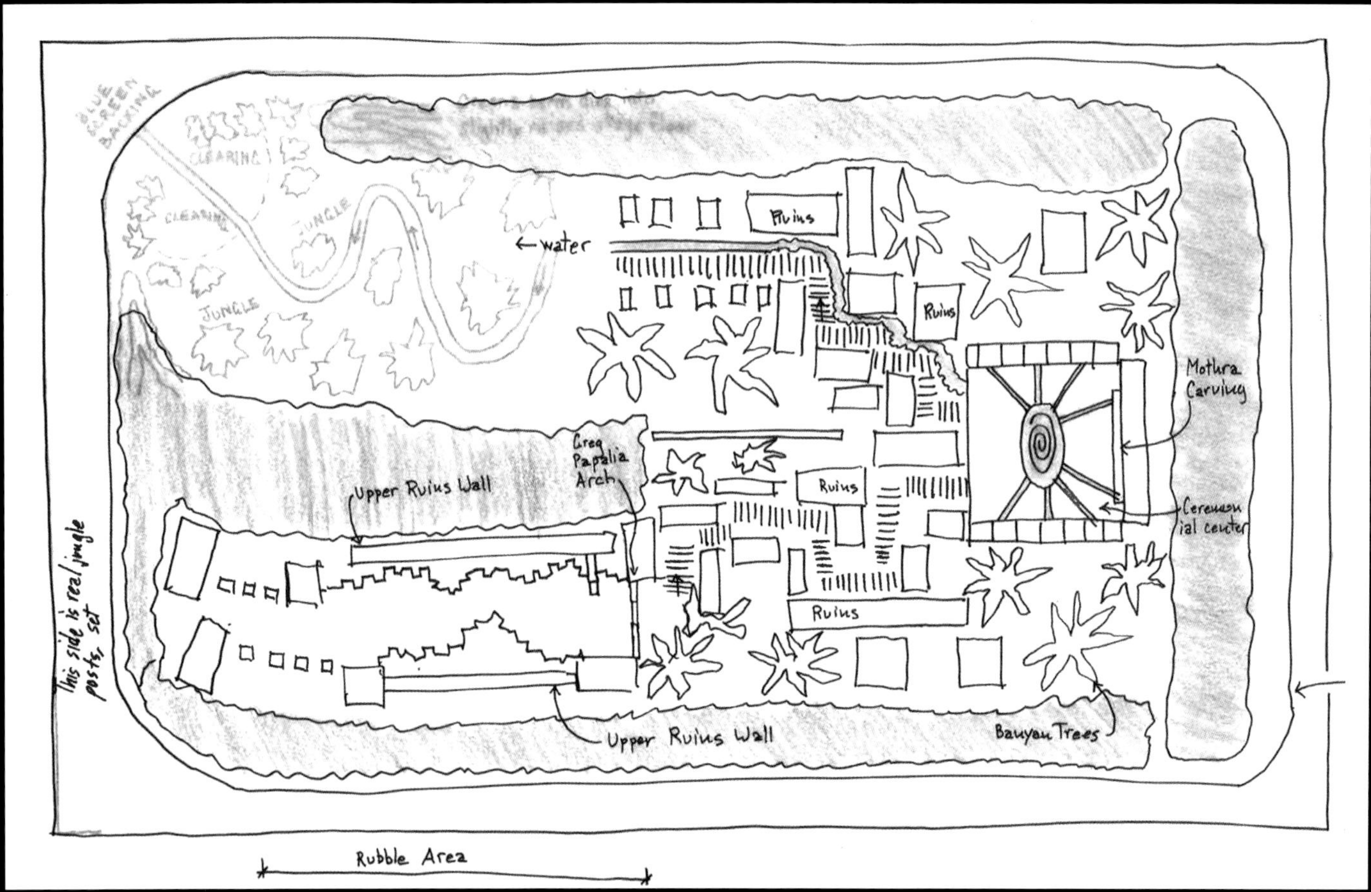

BLUE SCREEN BACKING
CLEARING
CLEARING
JUNGLE
JUNGLE
←water
Ruins
Ruins
Mothra Carving
Greg Papalia Arch
Upper Ruins Wall
Ruins
Ceremonial center
Ruins
This side is real jungle posts, set
Upper Ruins Wall
Banyan Trees
Rubble Area

No Lintels
wall w/ pilasters
Altar
Adding a base detail
Staircase edge a real thing
Expanding the
Runnel down the middle

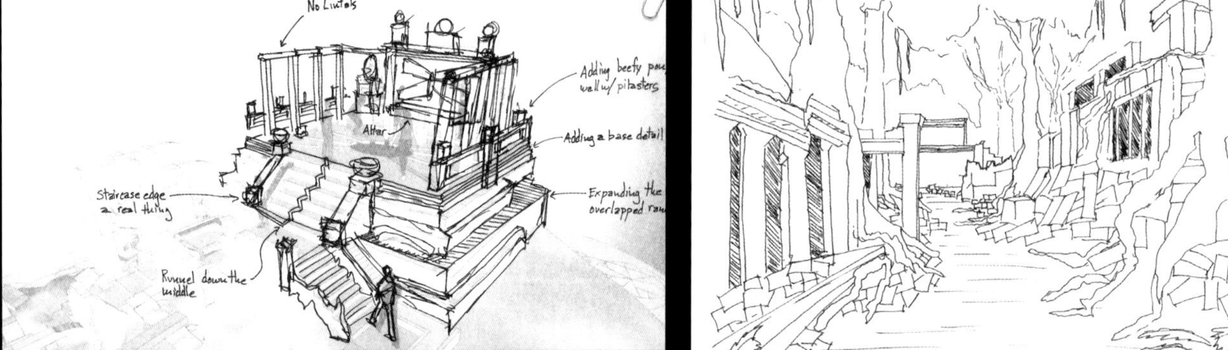

TOP This sketch by Tom Hammock shows the initial layout of the temple complex set on a soundstage.
RIGHT Two sketches of the Iwi ruins by Hammock.
OPPOSITE Flanked by huge, centuries-old trees, intricate steps lead to the Iwi ruins in this piece by Dean Sherriff.
FOLLOWING PAGES The team enters the temple complex, as illustrated by Sherriff. "We studied ancient stone structures, particularly in Peru, Malta, and Cambodia, as well as Nan Madol, Micronesia, before beginning the design of the temple," says Dean

THESE PAGES The nighttime concept for the bioluminescent Hollow Earth jungle as depicted by Dean Sherriff, who took inspiration from the vivid colors of glowworms.

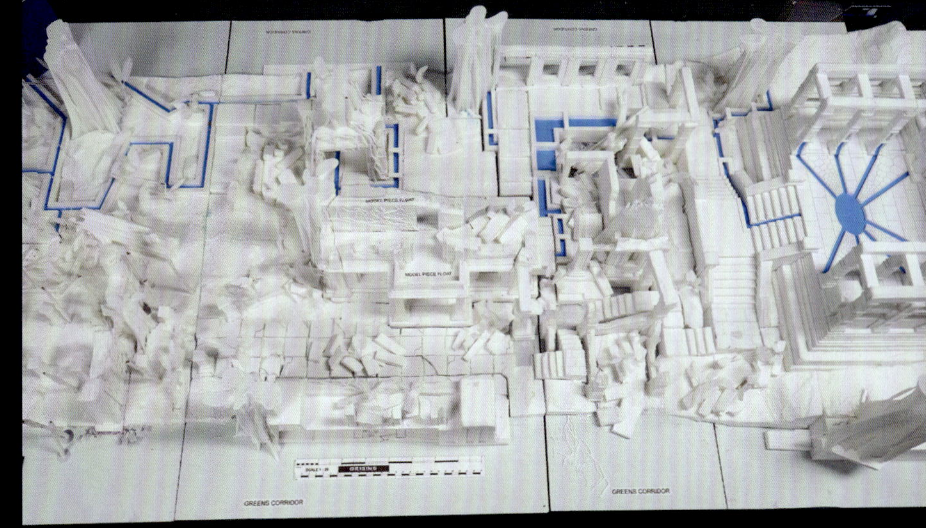

THIS PAGE A scale model of the Iwi ruins. "Adam Wingard and Tom Hammock love working with physical models to perfect a set," says supervising art director Richard Hobbs. "These let us specify the level of collapse and the placement of every tree root so the sculptors had a place to start working from."
OPPOSITE On set, the Iwi ruins come to life. "It was incredible just to see it slowly coming together," says Wingard. "I remember I walked in one day, when one of the sculptors was out there working on the trees, and what you don't realize is just to make one of those trees realistic . . . somebody's literally sitting there with this tiny tool, etching thousands of little lines in it to make it look randomized and real before they paint. And there's just so much detail that goes into creating something like this."

THE VEIL

THIS PAGE Two preliminary images by Michele Moen show a weblike veil, woven by Mothra, that spans the Hollow Earth jungle and hides Malenka from view. "The Titans weren't supposed to be able to see the web-like mesh, so it had to reflect jungle greenery to blend in, but it had to be somewhat visible in the illustration. The silk web refracted light, creating a shimmering rainbow of colors," says Moen. **OPPOSITE** The view through the veil to the Iwi valley and the Malenka crystal pyramids.

RIGHT In this concept by Ulrich Zeidler, the normal rules of physics don't apply in Hollow Earth, as the landscape curls upward near to where the H.E.A.V. 2.0 has landed.

PAGE 162 This concept depicts the massive pyramids at Malenka. "I had problems wrapping my head around this world a little bit in the beginning," says Dean Sherriff. "When you're looking at something triangular that's tapering away . . . it already has perspective. So how do you make it look big? That was the challenge with these pyramids . . . how to get the scale."

PAGE 163 TOP ROW These two concepts by Raj Rihal show a view of the pyramids from the ground. "It was a theme throughout the entire thing to have these very simple geometric shapes. That goes back to Adam [Wingard] and [Tom Hammock's] original influences of those '80s toy designs, which are very, very simplistic in shape. They have very basic geometric shapes with layered textures and colors," says Rihal.

PAGE 163 BOTTOM LEFT A wide perspective on Malenka by Zeidler.

PAGE 163 BOTTOM RIGHT A view of the mirrored pyramids by Dean Sherriff.

malenka

OPPOSITE Concept of a Malenka plaza shrine by Alex Moy.
TOP AND BOTTOM LEFT The spears held by the Iwi warriors are used both for protection and to operate Iwi technology.
TOP RIGHT Variations of Malenka plaza flagpoles by Moy.
ABOVE Additional shrine designs by Moy.

THESE PAGES Inspired by the vivid hues seen in many temples, Dean Sherriff's illustrations of the Iwi pyramids employ a repeating color scheme.
FOLLOWING PAGES The pyramid-shaped temples collide in this dynamic concept art by Sherriff.

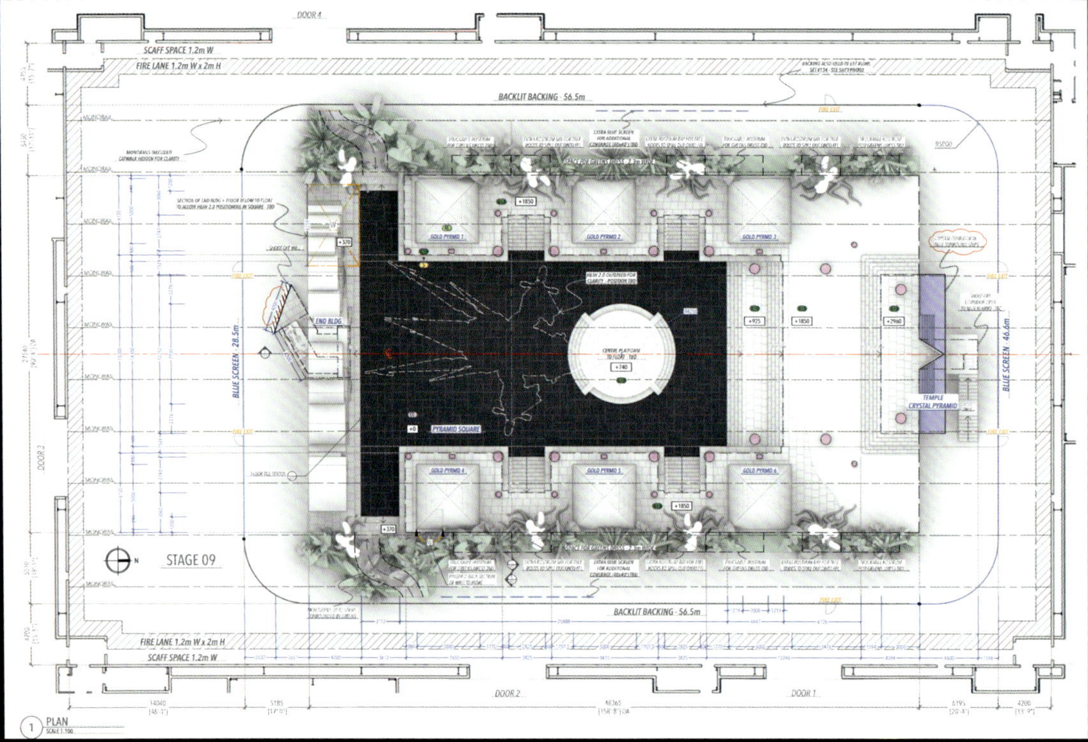
DOOR 4
SCAFF SPACE 1.2m W
FIRE LANE 1.2m W x 2m H
BACKLIT BACKING - 56.5m
GOLD PYRMID 1
GOLD PYRMID 2
GOLD PYRMID 3
END BLDG
BLUE SCREEN - 28.5m
BLUE SCREEN - 46.6m
PYRAMID SQUARE
TEMPLE
CRYSTAL PYRAMID
STAGE 09
BACKLIT BACKING - 56.5m
FIRE LANE 1.2m W x 2m H
SCAFF SPACE 1.2m W
DOOR 2
DOOR 1
PLAN

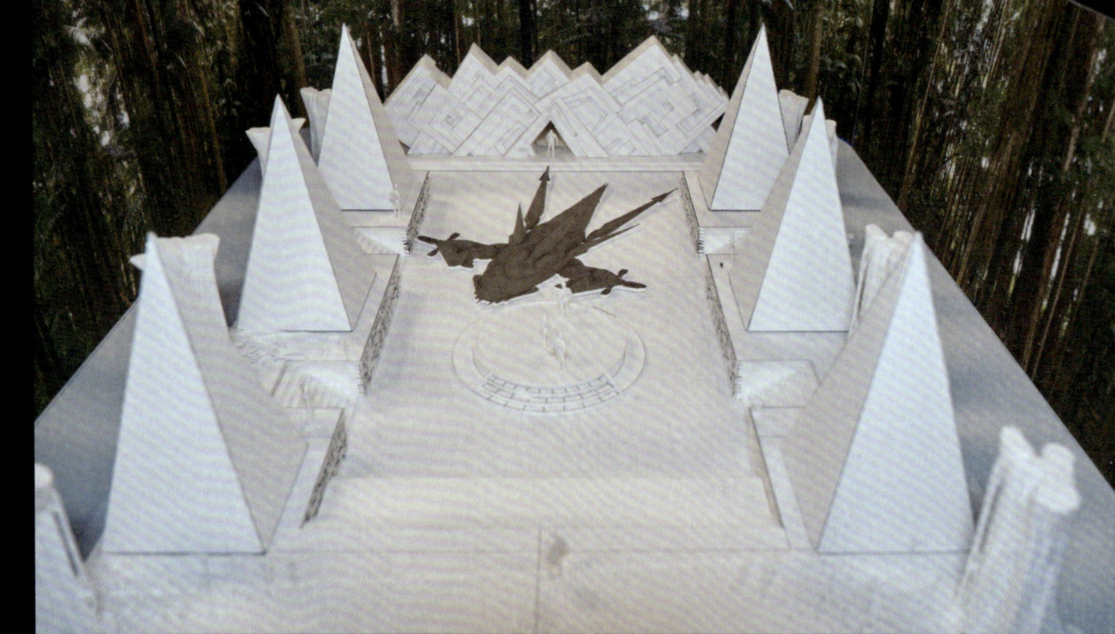

TOP Detailed schematic for the pyramid square by Rachel van Baarle and Matt Wynne.
RIGHT A model of the pyramid square used to work out the landing of the H.E.A.V.
OPPOSITE Constructed on a soundstage, the pyramid square takes shape. “This whole pyramid complex . . . we knew we needed to see some part of this Iwi civilization. But we knew we couldn’t build an entire city,” says Adam Wingard. “And so what we landed on was this complex, a meeting spot—an almost ceremonial area that’s at the base of the pyramid. We tried to make sure that everything here was believable.”

RIGHT In this chamber, Jia, Dr. Andrews, Bernie, and Trapper learn about the history of Hollow Earth's Titans. The completed set, built on the soundstage at Village Roadshow Studios, is pictured here. **OPPOSITE** Designs for intricate stone carvings showing the history of the Titans, as seen on the walls of the History Chamber, illustrated by Alex Moy.

ABOVE The Engineering Room cask features a pouring spout molded into the rim. "Once it was filled with liquid, we discovered that the cask was deceptively heavy, so for the cast to be able to pour the liquid accurately, we needed to add a spout," says illustrator Alex Moy.

OPPOSITE TOP ROW AND BOTTOM LEFT Three illustrations by Ulrich Zeidler show the Engineering Room.

OPPOSITE BOTTOM RIGHT An alternate version of the Engineering Room, where ancient Iwi technology uses liquid mercury to power huge machinery, here imagined by Matthew Cunningham.

PART VII

THE SKAR KING'S REALM

PART VII:

THE SKAR KING'S REALM

As Dr. Ilene Andrews leads the expedition into Hollow Earth, she and her team discover the Iwi civilization, led by a resplendent queen. At last, Jia is able to reconnect with her people. In a parallel storyline, Kong and Suko journey through this subterranean realm, eventually arriving at the Skar King's realm, where they encounter the tyrannical Titan, who has enslaved apes from Kong's species and holds Shimo captive. As he began to conceptualize this vast and varied landscape, director Adam Wingard thought of Hollow Earth in metaphorical terms.

"It's the inner cerebral realm for the monsters—it represents the emotional journey of Kong in a lot of ways," he says. "For example, in the beginning of the film, we really play up the spaciousness, the big loneliness, that it has. We really emphasize that during Kong's journey. And then, as he goes deeper and deeper into the subterranean realm, journeying to the Skar King's lair is really very much a descent into Hell. So the environments are always being dictated in an emotional way for Kong."

As Hammock points out, this geographical journey is a visual one as much as anything. "The lush, green world of Hollow Earth gives way to the black and red tones of [the Skar King's realm]. Aggressive, sharp shapes and a landscape of black dried lava speak to the danger and violence of the Skar King's realm. In this place, the ceiling of Hollow Earth hangs low to emphasize the prison-like aspect of this fierce world."

Wingard sees Hollow Earth like the underworld, with the Skar King as a devil-like figure and the apes he has enslaved as lost souls. "You could almost look at the tribe within Hollow Earth that Kong helps as being almost like ghosts," he says. "They're trapped in Hell with this devil character that's just making them toil away down there. And this movie is really about Kong saving them, redeeming them, and pulling them out of this place."

PREVIOUS PAGES In this illustration by Matt Allsopp, the captive Shimo is forced by the Skar King to battle Kong. Here, the Skar King's lackeys bring Shimo forth from her prison. **OPPOSITE** The Skar King's loyal servants, daubed with red clay in honor of their master, are depicted in this illustration by Ben Wootten.

THE GREAT APES

RIGHT Wētā Workshop design for a Great Ape.
OPPOSITE Close study of a female Great Ape and her infant, also by Wētā Workshop.
PAGE 184 LEFT This illustration was originally intended by artist Rob Bliss to be a take on the Skar King. However, when Adam Wingard went with another design, the director saw the potential in using this design for one of the Skar King's loyal guards.
PAGE 184 RIGHT AND PAGE 185 LEFT Two concepts by Wētā Workshop for One-Eye, a servant of the Skar King. "He's low on the totem pole," says Wingard. "And he wants to make a name for himself, so, he's willing to sell out anybody or anything. That's why he's the worst of all the Great Apes because he's a total sellout. He's just this mangy, awful little guy. And he wants to suck up to the Skar King."
PAGE 185 RIGHT One-Eye and his posse get the jump on Kong in these storyboards by Richard Bennett.

ONE-EYE AND THE LOYAL APES

BELOW A trio of designs for Great Apes loyal to the Skar King, created by Wētā Workshop.
RIGHT This illustration by Ben Wootten shows the moment before the Skar King battles Kong. Here, the Skar King emerges from his cave flanked by his bodyguards.
FOLLOWING PAGES In this piece by Wootten, the Skar King uses his Whipslash to wrest away Kong's axe.

The Skar King's Realm

THESE PAGES This concept artwork shows the Skar King's realm, including Shimo imprisoned behind a wall of flowing lava. "This was going to be a digital set . . . so it was a very specific location design that they wanted. Illustrations like these tend to be less about action and more about placement of things . . . to accomodate the action which will take place there," says illustrator Raj Rihal.

ENTER SHIMO

THESE PAGES In these illustrations by Matt Allsopp, Shimo is brought from her prison to fight Kong. This is an early iteration of Shimo where she is smaller than her final form. Kong is flanked by the iconic bone centerpiece of the arena made of ancient Godzilla-like species' rib bones.

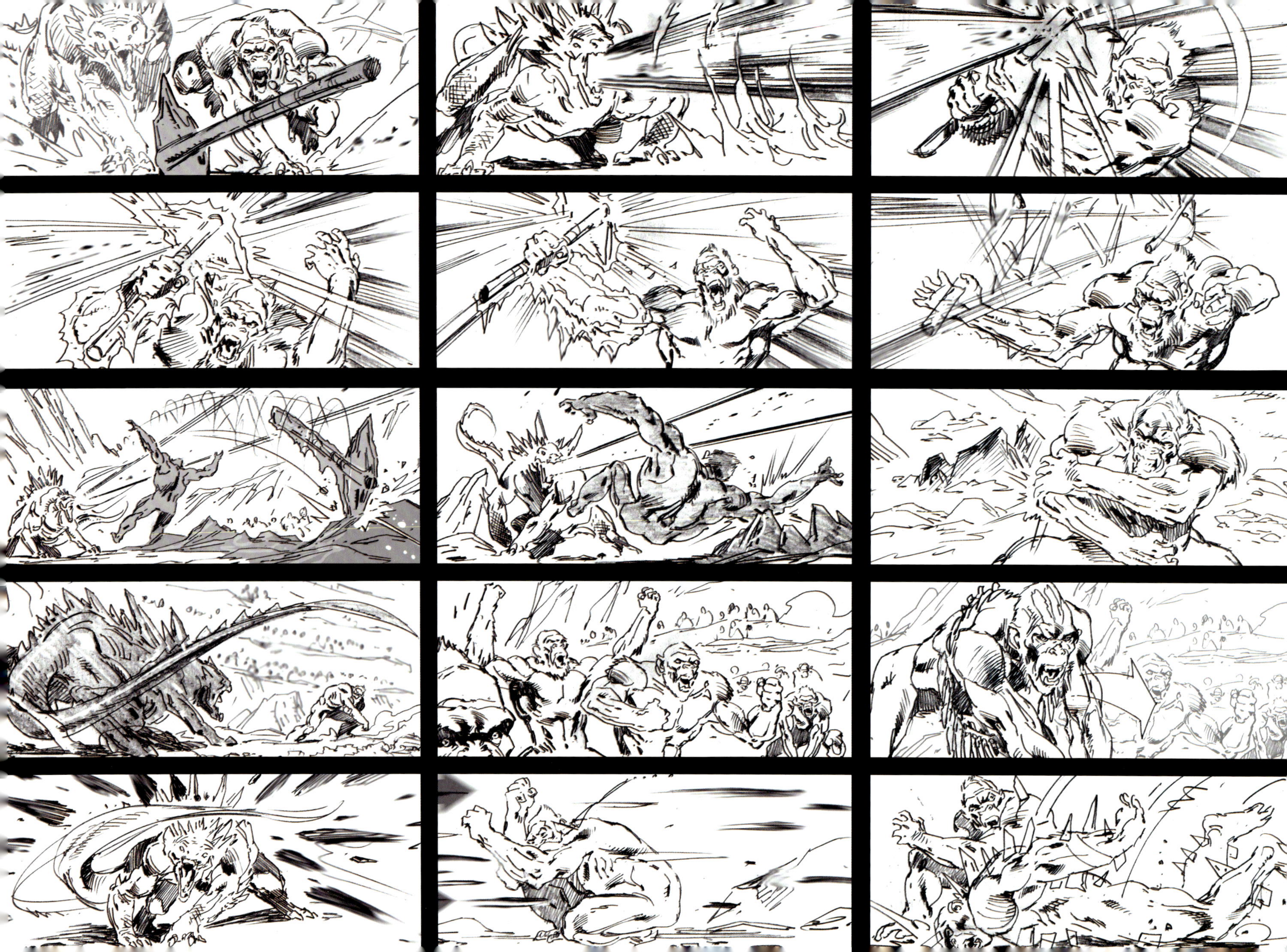

OPPOSITE Storyboards by Richard Bennett illustrate Kong's battle with the Skar King and Shimo. Disarmed by an icy blast from Shimo, Kong becomes an easy target for the Skar King. "Shimo is the Skar King's secret weapon. But he has mind control over her with this crystal that is on the Whipslash," says Bennett.
ABOVE Kong faces Shimo in the Skar King's arena, as shown by Matt Allsopp's concept art inspired by *Mortal Kombat*.

PART VIII

alliance

PART VIII:

ALLIANCE

As *Godzilla x Kong: The New Empire* reaches its final act, the Titans take each other on. "You need an epic final fight," suggests production designer Tom Hammock. "Fans want to see the Titans go at it." Leaving Hollow Earth, Kong surfaces through the sand, emerging near Egypt's majestic Pyramids of Giza. Sensing his presence, Godzilla jumps from the Rock of Gibraltar into the waters below, setting sail for North Africa and swimming up Egypt's famous Nile River as he prepares to face Kong. Adam Wingard knew that he wanted the film's electric final act to begin at one of the Seven Wonders of the World.

"I knew I wanted a battle in Egypt," says Wingard. "I just love the idea—'OK, here's a place that we know: the Pyramids of Giza. And this is what it looks like with Godzilla and Kong fighting each other at them!'" Wingard delighted in watching these Titans go head-to-head at this ancient Egyptian landmark. "The feeling I get sometimes is, it's like an adult version of being able to play with toys," he says. "It's the CGI character versions of them, and you get to smash them around and really let your imagination run wild."

That truly comes to pass, after Bernie and the Iwi Queen cause the pyramids of Hollow Earth to close, resulting in gravity inversion. Kong and Godzilla find themselves floating—and fighting—in a zero-gravity atmosphere in Hollow Earth. With these two heroes of the Monsterverse joined by Shimo and the Skar King, it was the culmination of an idea Wingard says he had introduced in *Godzilla vs. Kong*: "Trying to think of some new approaches we could have to a monster battle, I was, like, 'Well, we've never seen them in zero gravity.' And I always tend to like the idea of action scenes in a zero-gravity environment."

When the fight reemerges aboveground, the Titans land in Rio de Janeiro, Brazil. "We actually analyzed sixty cities," says Hammock, "because you need key elements, right? You have to have water for Godzilla. You generally want mountains. You need a downtown, where you have skyscrapers of an appropriate scale for Kong." The Brazilian city, with its beautiful beaches and urban sprawl, ultimately emerged as the right choice.

To protect civilization, Kong and Godzilla team up, paired against the Skar King and Shimo, like a Titan take on tag-team wrestling. After the concluding brawl between the titular Titans in *Godzilla vs. Kong*, it was time for a change. The production designer adds: "This time, Adam wanted to amp it up that much more and have a four-way fight. So I think it's just that much more exciting that you get four Titans fighting in the finale." With Shimo's ice breath causing snow to fall in the usually balmy South American city, "you get to see Rio in a way you've never seen it before," adds Hammock. "And you get a different view of the city and the scale because you're seeing it at the level of the Titans."

PREVIOUS PAGES In this piece by Manuel Plank-Jorge, Godzilla hears Kong's call and readies to leap from the Rock of Gibraltar into the Mediterranean Sea. **OPPOSITE** As Godzilla looks to annihilate Kong, he swims up the shallow Nile River, causing a destructive tidal wave, which is illustrated here by Plank-Jorge.

SOFITEL

THESE PAGES Two concept pieces by Manuel Plank-Jorge show Godzilla plunging into the water from the Rock of Gibraltar. "You're constantly asking, 'How do we get to see Godzilla and Kong doing things you've never seen before?' And I'd never seen Godzilla really launch himself off something into water before like that," the illustrator says. "So this was a fun opportunity to have him dive into the water. And what better place to do this than from the iconic Rock of Gibraltar?"

ABOVE Godzilla and Kong slug it out on the streets of Cairo in this illustration by Manuel Plank-Jorge.
OPPOSITE Another view of the tidal wave from Godzilla swimming

THESE PAGES Kong emerges from Hollow Earth at the pyramids of Giza. Holding his axe aloft, Kong calls for Godzilla while helicopters circle the scene.

HESE PAGES Two illustrations from Raj Rihal illustrate key moments
n Godzilla and Kong's brawl. Believing that Kong is a challenger for
odzilla's turf, the latter Titan draws him into a kinetic rematch.

LEFT Three dynamic illustrations from Raj Rihal visualize key beats in Godzilla and Kong's rematch. "Adam [Wingard] and Tom [Hammock] said, 'We're gonna have Kong and Godzilla fighting in Egypt. And we want to have the Pyramids.' So, I came up with action shots of the two interacting, like slamming against the pyramids. And I think that kind of set the tone, because they wanted it really big, with a lot of drama," says Rihal.

PAGE 204 These storyboards by Richard Bennett depict the moment that Jia breaks up the fight between Godzilla and Kong.

PAGE 205 The concluding moment of the duel is illustrated by Raj Rihal. "Jia is up there, waving a feather, so it's about scale," says Rihal. "And there's the humor in that, but we really wanted to see just how big Godzilla [is] in that moment. And I just wanted to capture how much that sand was just everywhere and swirling!"

THE BATTLE IN ZERO GRAVITY

THESE PAGES Now aligned, Godzilla and Kong take the fight to the Skar King, which leads to a zero-gravity showdown. In this illustration by Jared Krichevsky, Kong brings down his axe on the Skar King, while a Great Ape clashes with one of the tyrant's loyalists. "Adam and Tom gave me a sketch. They're, like, 'Give us this, but realized.' We wanted to see both sides of Hollow Earth—the guys fighting in the background, the rocks colliding, and then seeing [the Skar King and Kong] both together. It was awesome. But, man, that was a hard one to draw," says Krichevsky.

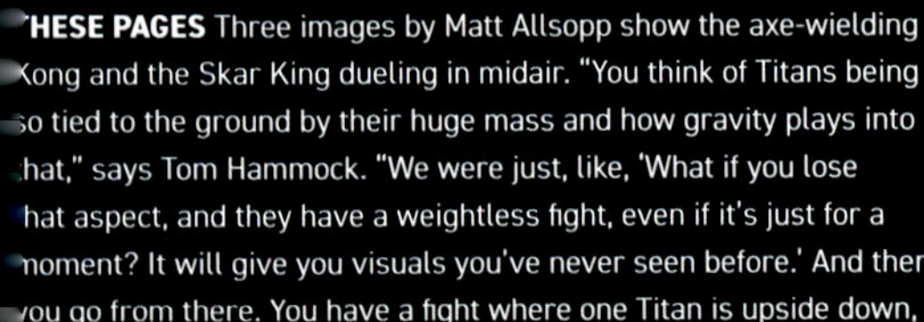

'HESE PAGES Three images by Matt Allsopp show the axe-wielding Kong and the Skar King dueling in midair. "You think of Titans being so tied to the ground by their huge mass and how gravity plays into hat," says Tom Hammock. "We were just, like, 'What if you lose hat aspect, and they have a weightless fight, even if it's just for a moment? It will give you visuals you've never seen before.' And then you go from there. You have a fight where one Titan is upside down,

THESE PAGES AND FOLLOWING PAGES In these illustrations by Matt Allsopp, Godzilla and Shimo duke it out in zero gravity.

RIO DE JANEIRO

THESE PAGES In this illustration by Alex Moy, the arrival of the four Titans in Rio de Janeiro is heralded by an unusual phenomenon: As Shimo and the three other Titans hurtle from Hollow Earth toward the ocean surface of the beachside city, Shimo's frosty powers cause the water to freeze.

FOLLOWING SPREAD Rio as it's never been seen before: under a blanket of snow with a frozen ocean. Moy strove to accurately capture Rio de Janeiro's famous landmarks in this illustration. "I spent some time delving into the famous landmarks and streets of Rio, poring over photographs, documentaries, drone footage, paintings, and so on," Moy says. "I was looking for anything that felt immediately recognizable as Rio to incorporate into the frames. It is a beautiful place architecturally, geographically, and culturally, so I wanted to understand the scale and presence of each landmark within the city in order to depict it accurately."

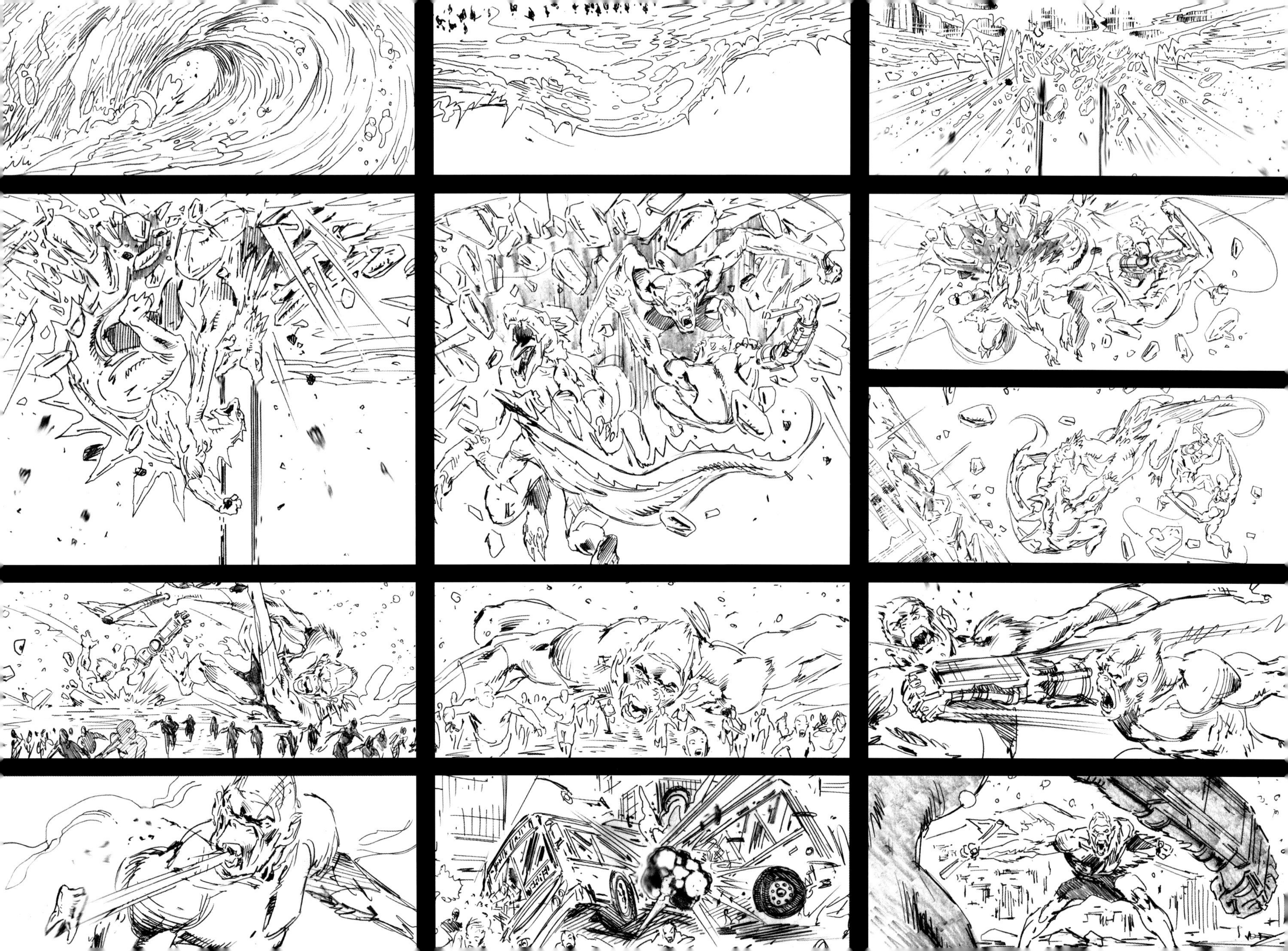

OPPOSITE Storyboards by Richard Bennett depict the moment that the four Titans burst from Hollow Earth and into Rio de Janeiro. Kong lands a right hook on the Skar King, who then spits out a tooth that obliterates a nearby bus.
ABOVE The four-way Titan fight as illustrated by Matt Allsopp, highlighting a unique vision of Rio with falling snow and an iceberg-choked ocean.

THESE PAGES Kong and Godzilla take on the Skar King and Shimo, respectively, among the landmarks of Rio in these illustrations by

CONCLUSION

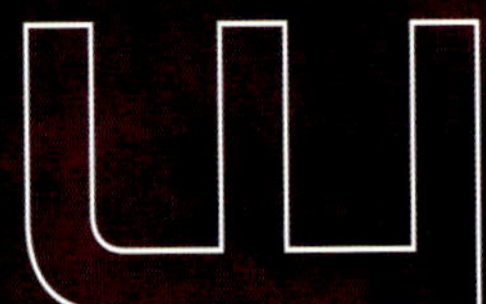

With *Godzilla x Kong: The New Empire*, the Monsterverse has evolved in extraordinary ways. "I think the way that we have expanded this series is by leaning into the fact that . . . this film, more than any of the others that's ever been made, including [*Godzilla vs. Kong*], proves that the Titans can tell their own story," says Adam Wingard. "And you don't always need a human being there to narrate what's going on; you can rely on nonverbal visual storytelling."

Wingard partly attributes this to the fact that the Titans in the Monsterverse are now so beloved. "These [characters] are so well understood by people that they can just exist, and we can follow them around and they can let their story unfold and it's not confusing to people. We understand what the Titans are thinking no matter what. To me, it's a big leap forward in this new, exciting direction, because there's almost no going back from here once you've proven that these movies can [include] almost eight-minute-long sequences . . . where there's not a human in sight."

Wingard is confident that visual effects technology is now advanced enough to support a Titan-centric direction. "The unlimited creativity that can be put into these sequences . . . there's nothing holding us back anymore. And so now going forward, it's going to be a whole new ballgame. And I think this is what people have always wanted from these movies. And I think now we're stepping into the territory that everybody's always suspected you can go into, but we've never seen before."

Putting the Titans front and center in such solo sequences, sans humans, isn't the only way *The New Empire* helped evolve the Monsterverse. "We expanded Hollow Earth into a fully realized world complete with an ecosystem, geology, life, and, of course, new Titans," says production designer Tom Hammock, alluding to the creation of the Skar King and Shimo. "Plus our two new Hollow Earth ships, weapons, and suits for humans to navigate that world." Wingard concurs. "We've gone all over Hollow Earth," he says. "We've explored all types of different scenarios and terrains."

The question remains, what next for the Monsterverse? "I think there's some obvious interesting possibilities and where to go from there," says Wingard, who has ideas sketched out in his mind. "There's a lot of Easter eggs in *The New Empire*. If you look into Bernie's apartment, there are some Easter eggs placed there in terms of where the series [might] head."

OPPOSITE The Rio brawl, seen from the point of view of a soldier aboard a helicopter, as conceived by artist Matt Allsopp.
FOLLOWING PAGES Kong and Suko traverse Hollow Earth in this illustration by Michele Moen.

PO Box 3088
San Rafael, CA 94912
www.insighteditions.com

Find us on Facebook: www.facebook.com/InsightEditions
Follow us on Instagram: @insighteditions

Trade ISBN: 979-8-88663-370-2
Limited Edition ISBN: 979-8-88663-371-9

Publisher: Raoul Goff
VP, Co-Publisher: Vanessa Lopez
VP, Creative: Chrissy Kwasnik
VP, Manufacturing: Alix Nicholaeff
Art Director: Matt Girard
Designer: Lola Villanueva
Editor: Harrison Tunggal
Editorial Assistant: Alecsander Zapata
Executive Project Editor: Maria Spano
Senior Production Manager: Greg Steffen
Senior Production Manager, Subsidiary Rights: Lina s Palma-Temena

Insight Editions would like to thank Mary Parent, Alex Garcia, Barnaby Legg, Robert Napton, Josh Parker, Brooke Hansohn, Anna Cook, Kristina Holliman, Sam O'Braitis, and Romy Schneider. In addition, we would like to extend a special thank-you to the many interviewees whose insights informed this book.

Replanted Paper

Insight Editions, in association with Roots of Peace, will plant two trees for each tree used in the manufacturing of this book. Roots of Peace is an internationally renowned humanitarian organization dedicated to eradicating land mines worldwide and converting war-torn lands into productive farms and wildlife habitats. Roots of Peace will plant two million fruit and nut trees in Afghanistan and provide farmers there with the skills and support necessary for sustainable land use.

Manufactured in Turkey by Elma Basim

10 9 8 7 6 5 4 3 2 1